# THE
# SIGNIFICANCE AND BASIC
# POSTULATES OF ECONOMIC
# THEORY

# THE
# SIGNIFICANCE
## AND
# BASIC POSTULATES
## OF
# ECONOMIC THEORY

BY

## T. W. HUTCHISON
M.A.

REPRINTS OF ECONOMIC CLASSICS

*Augustus M. Kelley, Bookseller*
*New York 1965*

" *Straightway one of those numberless unfortunates who are cursed with the mania for talking about things they do not understand comes forward with the discovery—lo the wonders of genius!—that pure economics is not applied economics, and concludes . . . that pure economics must be replaced by his gabble. Alas, good soul, mathematical economics helps at least to a rough understanding of the effects of the interdependence of economic phenomena, while your gabble shows absolutely nothing!* "

V. PARETO
The Mind and Society
(*Translated by* A. Livingston *and* A. Bongiorno)

# PREFACE

THIS book was written in 1936-37, since when there has been a great deal of change and decay which have much affected my views, though not so much, perhaps, on the fairly limited problems discussed here. There is no question of my re-writing the whole work, and I have little idea as to what would emerge if I attempted to do this. So if the book is to have another little run for Mr. Kelley's money, it seems that the best thing I can do, in this Preface, is to try to indicate, very briefly, how far I am now prepared to uphold the views expressed here against some of the main explicit criticisms, and contrasting or conflicting ideas, which have been put forward in recent years.

The first point made in this book and one that has attracted much criticism, concerns what Professor Popper has called the Demarcation Problem, or Demarcation Criterion for distinguishing "between the statements, or systems of statements, of the empirical sciences, and all other statements."[1] There are certainly crudities and inadequacies in my attempt to formulate and explain the, (or a), Demarcation Criterion (p. 6-p. 16),—(and I did not insist that my formulation gave "necessarily exactly the most suitable defining line between these two planes of science and non-science") (p. 12).[2] But I would hold that questions as to the best precise formu-

---

[1] v. British Philosophy in the Mid-Century, ed. C. A. Mace, p. 162.

[2] For example, I would not now use the heading (p. 6) "Scientific" and "Philosophical" Problems, but rather say "Scientific" and "Non-Scientific" Problems, or The Demarcation of Empirical Science. I would omit the words "resorts to" in the first sentence of section 3 (p. 10). I would not want to commit myself to saying that by the demarcation criterion the scientist can keep his results "pure" (p. 11), but simply—(say)—that it "can help him to keep his results distinct." I would omit the rather challenging quotation from Pareto (p. 13). And I would omit the remarks about the notion of metaphysical assumptions (p. 17).

vii

lation of the criterion are of less importance—(for the economist, at any rate, if not for the analytical philosopher)—
than the question of principle as to whether *any* such demarcation criterion has, or can have, a useful role in economics and the social sciences,—as some economists have denied. Was, or is, suggesting a criterion of this kind just a
fussy, bossy, governessy, "impatient" attempt to regulate or
legislate about economic studies, or to lay down obstructive
methodological rules or prescriptions? I don't think such a
suggestion was or is. Such a suggestion still seems as though
it might be useful or clarificatory in various ways.

Of course, in advocating a criterion of this kind, one is
simply making a proposal (p. 13) in a field in which—obviously—there can be no enforceable legislation. What the
recognition of such a criterion proposes is, in the first place,
that it is a useful question to ask or keep asking about statements or theories, especially if there is ambiguity or disagreement about them: "Can one describe what would constitute
an inter-subjective empirical test or refutation of this statement or theory, or how would one attempt to falsify it, or
carry out a test of it?" It suggests further that, if the statement or theory is, or is claimed to be, an empirical one, should
not every attempt be made to refute it, or bring it to a serious
test,—even though this may be practically impossible here
and now,—rather than to shield it from testing, or attempts
at testing or refutation? Raising and pressing such questions
can, it seems, be clarificatory and can contribute to diminishing the area of disagreement. What is being proposed is thus
not some kind of prohibition or veto, but that a useful, and
perhaps essential, step towards clarification and agreement
should, wherever possible, be taken.

The recognition of the (or a) demarcation criterion to mark
off the statements and theories of a "discipline" from a
"non-," or "un-discipline" seems specially and perennially
important for the social studies or sciences. In a very interesting autobiographical passage Professor Popper recently

explained how he "first began to grapple with the problem, *'When should a theory be ranked as scientific?'* or *'Is there a criterion of the scientific character or status of a theory?'* ... *I wished to distinguish between science and pseudo-science.'*[1] He explains how he was struck by a contrast between theories of physics and various theories of human behaviour, notably those of Marx, Freud, and Adler. It appeared that whereas a theory of physics *"is incompatible with certain possible results of observation,"* some Marxian and other theories "were compatible with the most divergent human behaviour so that it was practically impossible to describe human behaviour which could not be interpreted as being in agreement with these theories." Professor Popper goes on to describe the "conventionalist stratagems" and "rescuing operations" which "by introducing *ad hoc* some auxiliary assumption or by reinterpreting the theory *ad hoc* in such a way that it escapes refutation," enable its admirers to continue to uphold it.

Among my own grounds for trying to formulate a demarcation criterion, a primary one, specially relevant in the mid-thirties, was to be able to mark off statements and theories based on, or deriving from, a disciplined study, from the statements and theories of the undisciplined, pseudo-scientific, totalitarian ideologies, the rise of which I apparently regarded as "the most sinister phenomenon of recent decades" (p. 10).

Totalitarian and other comprehensive ideologies need not, intellectually, be taken so seriously in the Western world today. But pseudo-scientific political propaganda presented as, or more or less surreptitiously mixed in with, economic analysis, is not obviously on the decrease. In fact, contrasting political value-judgments, ambiguously inserted, seem recently to have played a considerable part in what Sir Robert Hall, President of the Royal Economic Society, describes as "the fact of the very wide differences of opinion which appear

---

[1] Op. cit., p. 155.

to exist between economists on quite fundamental aspects of policy.'' Sir Robert even goes on to argue that ''narrowing so far as possible the limits within which there is disagreement between economists can be done with any prospects of success only by appeals to experience.''[1] So narrowing the area of disagreement seems quite an urgent objective, and the (or a) demarcation criterion, and the critical questions which it prompts, can still play a useful clarificatory role here in separating value-judgments, and persuasive overtones and suggestions, from testable and falsifiable statements and theories.

A further useful function of the criterion of testability, or falsifiability, is that it helps one, or reminds one, to distinguish between, and keep distinguished, empirical statements and tautologies or definitions; that is, in the rough and ready terms of a quotation I used (p. 21), ''to keep questions of language separate from questions of fact.'' This kind of confusion then seemed to me rather widespread in economic controversies. It may be that even if emphasis on this distinction might perhaps have been relevant or justifiable a quarter of a century ago, the progress of analytical clarity has now rendered it unnecessary or pedantic, and hence reduced the usefulness of the (or a) demarcation criterion, and of the questions it prompts.

On the other hand, in the last (December 1959) number of the Economic Journal we find the President of the Royal Economic Society and Economic Adviser to Her Majesty's Government urging on members of the Society that confusion over just this distinction is ''a besetting sin of economists.''[1] More precisely, the sin is that ''of enumerating purely definitional relationships when they purport to be making statements about reality. . . . This sin is so pervasive that I almost wish that it were within our power to mark out in some way any economist who failed to use consistently the identity

---

[1] Economic Journal, Dec. 1959, p. 647 and p. 650.
[1] Op. cit., p. 651.

symbol when writing a definitional equation and to confine the use of the equals symbol to empirical relationships or hypotheses.'' So perhaps the (or a) demarcation criterion, and the questions it prompts, still may have a useful clarificatory function also in this direction.

This suggested criterion serves simply for distinguishing between empirical science and non-science. It does not distinguish between different branches or types of empirical science, or between the natural and social sciences. To advocate the criterion is in this sense ''naturalistic,'' in that it seems to imply that there is no significant, fundamental distinction between the epistemological characteristics of the social sciences, as distinct from the natural sciences. This is the reason for the most fundamental and comprehensive type of objection to the (or a) demarcation criterion, such as we suggest. It is held—(perhaps to a decreasing extent)—that empirical testability and falsifiability may provide a suitable criterion for the statements and theories of the natural sciences, but is quite inapplicable, or distorting, if applied to statements and theories characteristic of the social sciences. These are concerned with purposive, ''rational,'' problem-solving, human actions and their motives, statements about which cannot conceivably be tested or falsified empirically, since they rest on intuitive ''understanding,'' and introspection. This was the main basis for the criticisms of Professor F. H. Knight,[1] if I have understood him correctly. Of course I cannot re-argue this whole issue here, but it seems to me as definitely as it did twenty years ago that the crucial points in Professor Knight's case should be rejected.

However, my views have become considerably less ''naturalist,'' or less naively or crudely so, than they were twenty years ago. Differences between the natural and the social sciences seem more important and ineluctable than they did then. Indeed, though quite ready, for the most part, to accept

---

[1] Journal of Political Economy, Vol. 48, 1940, p. 1; reprinted in 'On the History and Method of Economics,' Chicago, 1956.

and rely on Professor Popper's anti-naturalist thesis in *The Poverty of Historicism*, I would not always want to go so far as he seems to go in denying significance to the differences between the natural and social sciences. The much greater difficulty in securing adequate and convincing tests for statements and theories in human and social studies is, and it seems will always remain, a source of important differences. But these are differences of degree—though vital and consequential differences of degree—and not of principle. The doctrines of a fundamental discontinuity in epistemological criteria between the study of nature and the study of man do not seem acceptable.[1]

Above all, the rejection of the demarcation criterion of intersubjective testability and falsifiability—as, for example, by Professor Knight,—seems to leave subjective feelings of certainty, or what Professor Popper calls "psychologism," as the sole, hopelessly inadequate, basis for statements and theories in the social field, with no principle for marking them off or trusting them more rationally, as based on an intellectual discipline, than the utterances of the soothsayer, the ideologist and the crank. Moreover, a process essential, or invaluable, for diminishing and limiting the area of disagreement would disappear.

At this point I would like to mention briefly Professor Friedman's attack on the testing of "assumptions" of theories in his well-known paper "The Methodology of Positive Economics." Generally speaking, Professor Friedman strongly upholds the empirical testability and testing of statements and theories in economics, but holds that tests should or can only be applied to "predictions" and not to "assumptions." His thesis is thoroughly "naturalist" in that he implies no distinction, much less some fundamental epistemological discontinuity, between the natural and social sciences —in contrast with Professor Knight. Without specifically

---

[1] C.f. M. Polanyi, The Study of Man, Chicago, 1959.

advocating the testing of the "assumptions" of theories,—whatever precisely is to be understood by this term,—one can hold that empirical evidence, and indeed every sort of relevant test, should be brought to bear wherever possible in economics, and in particular that necessary "assumptions" should, in any case, be testable, if not actually tested or practically testable on the spot.

I, personally, have had some difficulty in appreciating Professor Friedman's argument, because the target of his attack does not seem to be quite clearly set out. At one point he states that "the very concept of the 'assumptions' of a theory is surrounded with ambiguity."[1] But he does not seem completely to have dispelled this ambiguity before attacking so forthrightly the testing of the "assumptions" of a theory. The possibility that his argument is to a considerable extent terminological seems to be suggested by his usually—(though not always)—writing of "assumptions" in inverted commas. Indeed, he goes so far as to question whether theories should be said to have "assumptions"—(in the phrase "in so far as a theory can be said to have 'assumptions' at all"[2]). (Incidentally, those who have followed Professor Friedman, or cited his doctrine approvingly, seem to have taken no notice of his inverted commas and his uncertainty as to the concept of the "assumptions" of a theory.)

Needless to say, if theories have not got, or do not require "assumptions," it is at least irrelevant to try to attempt or require any testing of them. There can only be a question as to the legitimacy, relevance, or desirability of testing, as far as is practically possible, such "assumptions"—if any—as are actually required by theories. In fact, Professor Friedman, after blasting the testing of "assumptions," or demands regarding the "realism" of assumptions, seems to reintroduce these very notions under other names. Professor Friedman begins by stressing that "full and comprehensive evi-

[1] v. Essays in Positive Economics, Chicago, 1950, p. 23.
[2] Op. cit., p. 14.

dence" is vital "in constructing hypotheses," which must be "consistent with the evidence at hand."[1] He goes on to hold that the "assumptions of a theory" are often "an economical mode of describing or presenting a theory." He also holds that "assumptions" have the necessary role of "specifying the conditions under which the theory is expected to be valid." "The assumptions of a theory" also may "facilitate an indirect test of the hypothesis by its implications."[2] It is very difficult to see how these "roles" of "assumptions" (as Professor Friedman calls them) could be carried out *without* what might be reasonably described as a concern for the "realism," or the testing (where practically possible), of the "assumptions" of a theory.

Otherwise, Professor Friedman's account of scientific explanation or prediction seems inadequate.[3] Simply to observe that a particular rise in price was followed by a fall in the quantity demanded—(without checking on what had happened to tastes, incomes, other prices etc., which might have been changing considerably,)—could, by itself, have little or no significance for any "scientific" explanation of price changes, or theory of price. Even though Professor Friedman may prefer some other terminology, this checking reasonably could be—(and surely is sometimes)—described as being based on a concern for the realism, or the testing, of the "assumptions" of a theory.

As regards what has been called "indirect testing," I would like to requote the following passages: (p. 9 and p. 19 note 6) "Propositions must conceivably be capable of empirical testing or be reducible to such propositions by logical or mathematical deduction . . . a scientific proposition may not itself be empirically testable directly, but may be reducible by

---

[1] Op. cit., p. 12 and 13.

[2] Op. cit., p. 23.

[3] See E. Rotwein, "On the Methodology of Positive Economics," Quarterly Journal of Economics, November 1959, p. 554 ff; and T. C. Koopmans, Three Essays on the State of Economic Science, New York, 1957, p. 137-141.

direct deduction to an empirically testable proposition or
propositions." That is, one can leave one assumption at a
time, or one part of a hypothesis at a time, to be "indirectly"
tested, by testing a conclusion that follows logically from it.
*and* any other assumption with which it is combined to yield
this conclusion. But I certainly would not agree that one
"need not worry or be very particular" about a number of
the assumptions of a theory (or of the separate parts of a
hypothesis).[1] If some uninstructed critic pointed to a rise in
price being followed by a rise in quantity demanded, without
"worrying or being very particular" about what had happened to consumers' objectives, tastes, expectations, incomes
or other prices, and he then triumphantly claimed that one of
the most solid of economic generalizations had been falsified,
he would be dismissed as a philistine ignoramus (or a naive
empiricist). It really will not do for economists now to claim
it as a demonstration of superior methodological wisdom, rising above the naive demands of "ultra-empiricism," to regard the generalization as scientifically corroborated whenever a rise in price is actually followed by a fall in the quantity demanded, without "worrying or being very particular"
about what had happened to consumers' objectives, tastes,

---

[1] Professor Machlup describes as an "ultra-empiricist" one who
"insists on the independent verification of all assumptions, hypothetical
as well as factual, perhaps even of each intermediate step in the analysis," (The Problem of Verification in Economics, Southern Economic
Journal, July 1955, p. 7). I think the above quotations show that I
am not and was never, an "ultra-empiricist" in this sense—as Professor
Machlup alleged. If, however, to reject completely a passage such as
the following is to stamp oneself an "ultra-empiricist," I hasten to
accept the description: "To summarize: We need not worry about
independent verifications of the fundamental assumption, the Assumed
Type of Action; we need not be very particular about the independent
verifications of the other intervening assumptions, the Assumed Conditions, because judgment based on casual empiricism will suffice for them;
we should insist on strict independent verifications of the assumption
selected as Assumed Change and of the conclusion derived as Deduced
Change; not that the theory would be wrong otherwise, but it cannot be
applied unless the phenomena to which it is supposed to apply are identi-
fiable. *Simultaneous verifications of Assumed Change and Deduced
Change count as verification—in the sense of non-disconfirmation—of the
theory as a whole.*"

expectations, incomes and other prices, that is, without any attempt at "testing assumptions."

As Koopmans has put it: "We have to exploit all the evidence we can secure, direct and indirect. If, in comparison with some other sciences, economics is handicapped by severe and possibly unsurmountable obstacles to meaningful experimentation, the opportunities for direct introspection by, and direct observation of, individual decision-makers are a much needed source of evidence which in some degree offsets the handicap. We cannot really feel confident in acting upon our economic knowledge until its deductions reconcile directly observed patterns of individual behavior with such implications for the economy as a whole as we find ourselves able to subject to test."[1]

For analyzing the statements of economists I proposed and used a two-fold classification, or dichotomy, between testable, falsifiable, empirical statements on the one hand, and tautologies on the other. This was proposed simply as convenient for the methodological analysis of statements in economics (p. 27). It may well be far from adequate for the philosopher or the student of morals or politics, for example, where there may be a more varied range or statements to analyze. But my classification would certainly be misleading and inadequate if there was a range of important statements used in economics which could not be regarded as either empirical, testable and falsifiable on the one hand, or tautological on the other.

Philosophical arguments in general terms that such a classification is inadequate, are not very convincing, or even reasonably clear, without satisfactory examples. What is wanted, —all that is wanted,—are a few quite clearly set out counterexamples of statements which do not fit this classification. I do not think such examples have been established. Examples have been sought in three directions, and not only is each one by itself fairly unsatisfactory, but they contrast oddly with one another.

[1] Op. cit., p. 140.

(1) In the first place, as argued (p. 46-47 note 7), I do not regard the Kantian category of synthetic *a priori* statements as playing a role in economics. I will not argue this further here.

(2) An entirely different kind of example for the inadequacy of my classification has recently been put forward by Messrs. Klappholz and Agassi: that of statements qualified by unspecified *ceteris paribus* assumptions (e.g. *"ceteris paribus* the imposition of a tax on cigarettes will raise their price"). [1] Messrs. K. and A. claim that I must be admitting the inadequacy of my classification in admitting that such statements may be either empirical or tautological, and therefore are not, as they stand, definitely one or the other. My main conclusion (p. 162) about *ceteris paribus* assumptions was that they are "frequently hopelessly ambiguous," (and hopelessly ambiguous not simply as to whether they are empirical or tautological). Let some attempt be made to specify the content of *ceteris paribus* and in my opinion such statements will emerge as one or the other, empirical or tautological. It does not seem to me a serious weakness of a classification such as I was adopting, that it cannot deal with "hopelessly ambiguous" statements. Certainly it cannot deal with statements such as "Assuming --- . . . ---, the imposition of a tax on cigarettes will raise their price," or "Messrs. K. and A. are --- . . . ---," which certainly are not testable or falsifiable as they stand and cannot certainly be said to be tautologies either. I think I can reasonably claim that my classification was simply concerned with reasonably unambiguously formulated statements, and excluded "hopelessly ambiguous" ones. However, if Messrs. K. and A. wish to classify the statements of economics into (1) empirical statements, (2) tautologies, and (3) hopelessly ambiguous statements, thus adding a third category to mine, I would not object. I simply hope that it is not excessively complacent if this does not seem to me to

---

[1] *Economica*, Feb. 1959, p. 63.

establish some sinister, restrictive inadequacy in the dichotomy which I adopted.

(3) The third example of the inadequacy of the classification I used seems to be represented by only a single definite statement, and that is the generalization about maximizing conduct by the consumer, and more especially by the entrepreneur, which I described as "the fundamental assumption." I think it must be clear that in describing this one particular assumption or statement as "fundamental." I was not ascribing to it any special, unique epistemological qualities, but simply implying that it was very frequently used in the analysis of firms and households. However, Professor Machlup,—(who seems to wish to combine both the Knightian objections to our demarcation criterion, with Friedman's objections to the testing of "assumptions,")—apparently regards "fundamental assumptions" as significantly numerous and as having some special epistemological status. But as regards further examples of "fundamental assumptions" he explains simply that "it all depends on what one regards as fundamental,"[1] which does not seem to help forward very far the process of clear exemplification. If it all depends on what assumptions one regards as fundamental, what if one does not, and need not, regard *any* assumptions in economics as "fundamental" in any special epistemological sense? And, anyhow, what are the characteristics which entitle one to regard an assumption as "fundamental"? Is it simply frequency of use, and if so just how much frequency? Is the assumption that, subject to certain restrictions, firms maximize their turnover, a "fundamental assumption"?

Professor Machlup, in fact, does not give any other definite example except that "perhaps" the technological assumption that only limited outputs can be obtained from given resources should be called fundamental, which is of some interest because it at least separates "fundamental assump-

---

[1] Southern Economic Journal, April 1956, p. 485.

tions'' from those concerned with introspection or purposive action.

Professor Machlup very well exemplifies the fog of ambiguity surrounding this one definite example of a ''fundamental assumption,'' by pointing out the number of names or descriptions which have been suggested for it: ''Various names have been suggested for the fundamental postulates of economic theory: 'economic principle,' 'maximization principle,' 'assumption of rationality,' 'law of motivation,' and others. And their logical nature has been characterized in various ways: they are regarded as 'self-evident propositions,' 'axioms,' 'a priori truths,' 'truisms,' 'tautologies,' 'definitions,' 'rigid laws,' 'rules of procedure,' 'resolutions,' 'working hypotheses,' 'useful fictions,' 'ideal types,' 'heuristic mental constructs,' 'indisputable facts of experience,' 'facts of immediate experience,' 'data of introspective observation,' 'private empirical data,' 'typical behavior patterns,' and so forth.''[1]

To me it seems highly unsatisfactory that economists should frequently make use of a statement or assumption when it is not clear whether it represents, for example, a tautology or definition, a fact of immediate experience, or a typical behavior pattern. This introduces an element of hopeless ambiguity into any theory in which such an assumption is used, about which I think it was justifiable to complain (p. 83-4); as it was also justifiable to emphasise the crucial significance for the fundamental assumption, and theories based on it, of the introduction of uncertainty (p. 84-94).

But perhaps, after all, it can now be agreed that the single example of a fundamental assumption *can* be fitted into my twofold classification as an empirical, falsifiable generalization. For although at one point Professor Machlup stated that ''fundamental assumptions are not directly testable and

---

[1] 'The Problem of Verification in Economics,' Southern Economic Journal, July 1955, p. 16.

cannot be refuted by empirical investigation,"—(though they are subject to a requirement of "understandability,") —he later concluded that it *was* "practically possible" to test directly the assumption of profit maximization, and added that in a number of cases it would be found to be refuted: "The assumption of consistently profit maximizing conduct is contrary to fact.''[1] That this "fundamental assumption" should be regarded as a testable, falsifiable, empirical generalisation,—(and as one which has been or could be actually falsified)—is exactly what I would want to say about it. I would merely wish to add that if a theory employing this assumption, or a hypothesis of which it was a component part, was being used for a scientific explanation of a sequence of events, it would be methodologically unwise, or complacently uncritical, not to worry about obtaining such evidence as was obtainable, as to whether in the case in question it was true or false; and it would be culpable negligence, if not only one did not "worry" about this assumption, but also, at the same time, was "not very particular" about other assumptions with which it was combined.

To summarize: I cannot regard these three types of examples—(Kantian synthetic *a priori* statements, unspecified *ceteris paribus* assumptions, and the assumption of profit maximization)—as demonstrating the serious inadequacy of the twofold classification or dichotomy which I employed. Moreover, those upholding the importance of a third type of statement apparently disagree completely as to the nature of this third type, and perhaps, or even probably, would reject one another's examples.

But by all means let us have some further cases. I hope, in fact, that the foregoing arguments may stimulate the working out of some clearer examples, so that the sort of classification I worked with can be elaborated, refined and im-

---

[1] Compare Southern Economic Journal, July 1955, p. 11, and April 1956, p. 488.

proved.[1] Perhaps I concentrated too exclusively on fitting
economic statements into one or other of these two categories,
because of what seemed to me the dogmatic and extreme
*a priorism* of Professor Mises, which was much more influ-
ential in the thirties.

My one request is for a number of clear examples. After
all, I think it would be agreed that one had only to take up
a book of principles, or a textbook, and one could, without
any shadow of ambiguity or disagreement, point immediately
to numerous examples of empirical statements and of tautologies. One might also, in some books, be able to point to a
number of "hopeless ambiguities," but one could justifiably
ask, either that these should be removed, or that some attempt
at clarification be made, in which case I would predict that
they would fall into one or other of the two categories I used.

As regards Chapter V on introspection, utility, social utility etc., this was written before the articles launching the
New Welfare Economics appeared. For what the point is
worth, it still seems right, on balance, to have held that inter-
personal comparisons of utility are not "illegitimate," and
that they do not necessarily involve value-judgments (p. 143-
153). But certainly I seem, to some extent, to have shared
the illusion that this argument had, or could have, vital significance for economists' conclusions about economic policy,
which it does not possess.

I also think that it was right, so far as the point goes, to
argue that what is called "welfare economics" can "be just
as positive as the other parts of economics" (p. 153), or at
any rate no more "normative," and that it can be "scientific"

---

[1] There seems, for example, to be something indistinct and obscure
about the concept of "*conceivable*" falsifiability or testability, though
this particular point does not seem to worry my critics. However, I cannot understand Messrs Klappholz and Agassi when they write (op. cit.,
p. 63): "One can imagine a factually false statement which is irrefut-
able. Such a statement would '*forbid* ... [some] conceivable occurrence,'
and yet would not be 'conceivably falsifiable by observation.' " To me
this is a direct contradiction in terms. But whether this has any relevance for any statements in economics seems to me doubtful.

in the same sense as medicine is "scientific"—(as, for example, Reder, and others have held). However, regarding the problem of value-judgments it does seem not a little naive to have considered the controversy to be "very nearly played out." (p. 154) In fact, I hope to publish something on this very problem shortly. But I would plead that the demarcation criterion on which I had earlier insisted provides much help in clarifying the problems of value-judgments. For the rest, the platitudes about the political elements in, or effects of, economic policies still seem just worth repeating. Indeed they may be coming into fashion, and they certainly carry more weight as problems of growth become more important.[1]

As regards the Appendix, I still think that the quotations cited in Note 1, which were its starting point, are quite preposterous. There are, however, one or two historical generalisations in this appendix to which I would not now subscribe. But the main point seems to have been that the arguments of the economist, and above all of the *a priori* economic theorist, can have very little weight in deciding the issues of capitalism versus socialism, which are, above all, political issues, which should be argued, on either side, in explicitly political terms. This again seems now to be a platitude, though still a sometimes disregarded platitude. But I do not think it can have been quite so platitudinous in the thirties, judging by the various quotations cited. Again to quote Professor Koopman's: "Our economic knowledge has not yet been carried to the point where it sheds much light on the core problem of the economic organization of society: the problem of how to face and deal with uncertainty. In particular, the economics profession is not ready to speak with anything approaching scientific authority on the economic aspects of the issue of individual versus collective enterprise which divides mankind in our time. Meanwhile, the best safeguard against overestimation of the range of applicability of economic

---

[1] C.f. J. R. Hicks, Essays in World Economics, Oxford, 1959, p. viii-p. xiv.

propositions is a careful spelling out of the premises on which they rest. Precision and rigor in the statement of premises and proofs can be expected to have a sobering effect on our beliefs about the reach of the propositions we have developed."[1]

T. W. HUTCHISON
Charlottesville, Va.
May 1960

---

[1] Op. cit., p. 147.

# PREFACE

It has usually seemed to me helpful in trying to appreciate a book which professes to be in some sense scientific, to be able to locate clearly how its conclusions stand *vis-à-vis* those of other writers on the subject, and to be able to perceive how its conclusions fit in, and how, if at all, they modify the impersonal " organon " of the science. Despite the paradoxical sound of the assertion, too much " originality "—or at any rate too much of the appearance of it—in many cases seems probably to be a dangerous fault in a scientific work; this must, nearly always, have emerged from the controversies and particular immediate problems of the science itself, and its arguments and message can only stand out more clearly if this setting and background is fully sketched in.

I have therefore made in this book extensive references to and quotations from other writers to whom I am either indebted or would have been indebted had I happened to read their works earlier. It seemed to me, further, more impressive and convincing, either in bringing support for my own conclusions or in the expositions of doctrines that seemed to me to be criticisable, to cite the actual words of authoritative writers. This procedure is certainly exposed to the possible danger of misquotation or misrepresentation. I very much hope that this has not occurred and I have done my best to avoid it. With regard to the quotation from works in a foreign language, in the text, where the quotation was particularly relevant to the understanding of the argument, I have undertaken a translation myself when an official translation has not been available. In the notes such passages are left in their original French or German.

This essay was virtually completed in the summer of 1937. Since then a number of important new works, particularly on the subject of economic fluctuations, have appeared of which it has not been possible to take full account here. I have, however, tried to indicate some of the more conspicuous points of agreement or disagreement. It is perhaps not too venturesome to claim that the present trend of Economics seems to be in the same direction as the point of view this book tries to establish.

I am grateful to the editors of the *Review of Economic Studies* and the *Zeitschrift für Nationalökonomie* for permission to make use of earlier formulations of parts of Chapters II., IV., and of the Appendix which appeared in their pages.

I began first to be interested in the problems discussed in this book while a pupil of Mrs. Robinson of Cambridge, and I should like, in conclusion, to acknowledge my general indebtedness to the incomparable training in and stimulus to economic thinking which I then received.

T. W. HUTCHISON

Bonn am Rhein
*February* 1938

# CONTENTS

CONTENTS

# I

# INTRODUCTION

1. "*The time has come to speak of fundamental things. . . . The methodological problem is, in great measure, the real problem.*"

J. ACKERMANN
Annual Survey of Economic Theory
Econometrica, **1936**

2. "*Wer ernstlich und ehrlich an Spezialproblemen der ökonomischen Theorie gearbeitet hat, wird zugeben müssen, dass man hierbei heute immer noch trotz aller Fortschritte der Theorie in ganz wesentlichen Punkten auf ebenso krasse wie weittragende Gegensätze der Meinungen bezüglich der allgemeinen Grundprobleme stösst, welche jede Übereinstimmung in der Lösung der Spezialprobleme zu einem Ding der Unmöglichkeit machen.*"

L. SCHÖNFELD
Grenznutzen und Wirtschaftsrechnung

3. "*If there are some subjects on which the results obtained have finally received the unanimous assent of all who have attended to the proof, and others on which mankind have not yet been equally successful ; on which the most sagacious minds have occupied themselves from the earliest date, and have never succeeded in establishing any con-*

1

*siderable body of truths, so as to be beyond denial or doubt ; it is by generalising the methods successfully followed in the former enquiries, and adapting them to the latter, that we may hope to remove this blot on the face of science.*"

J. S. MILL
System of Logic

4. "*Eine Wirklichkeitswissenschaft nämlich kann gar nichts anderes liefern als Beschreibungen und Erklärungen. . . . Wer etwas anderes von ihr verlangt, die mitteilbare Erkenntnisse liefern soll, der wendet sich gleichsam an die falsche Instanz. Eine Wissenschaft ist kein Inbegriff von Heilspredigten oder Erlösungsbotschaften oder rationalisierten Mythen oder Gedankendichtungen in Prosa, die auf Affektprojektionen und deren Pseudorationalisierung basieren. Sondern sie ist ein Inbegriff wenigstens im Prinzip erfahrungsmässig nachprüfbarer Aussagen nebst den dazu gehörenden Beobachtungen, Experimenten und kalkülmässigen Umformungen. Richtig ist nur, dass man, um überhaupt eine Wirklichkeitswissenschaft aufstellen und weiter entwickeln zu können, gewisser aktivistischer, auch gefühlsmässiger Antriebe bedarf, und dass also natürlich nicht aus Wissenschaft eine Wissenschaft zustande kommt, was manche Ideologen zu vermuten scheinen.*"

W. DUBISLAV
Die Definition

2

# I

# INTRODUCTION

## 1. THE PRESENT POSITION OF ECONOMIC " METHODOLOGY "

THE purpose of this essay is to help in elucidating the significance of that body of " pure theory " the possession of which distinguishes Economics from the other social sciences. It is concerned, therefore, to arrive at a clear definition of " pure theory " enabling one to mark off clearly propositions which belong to " pure theory " from those that do not, to investigate the source of the validity of these propositions, to clarify their relation to the assumptions or postulates on which they rest, including, in particular, the " ceteris paribus " assumption, and finally to clarify these assumptions themselves by analysing the main concepts (for example, " equilibrium ", " expectation ", " sensible " or " rational conduct ", " utility "), which they contain.

Despite the quantity of literature on such fundamental problems as these, few economists—least of all probably those like Kaufmann, Mackenroth, Morgenstern, Myrdal, and Robbins who in recent years have particularly contributed to their discussion—would claim that they are satisfactorily and definitively settled, even with that relative definitiveness which is the most that any scientist claims for his results.

3

The central conclusion of this essay has been advanced over and over again throughout the history of Economics. For the difficulty is not that of finding some new theory or standpoint—*on ne saurait rien imaginer de si étrange et si peu croyable, qu'il n'ait été dit par quelque philosophe*—but that of bringing conclusive and definitive arguments in favour of one as against the others—" conclusive ", that is, not necessarily *absolutely* (whatever that would mean), but according to some agreed scientific criterion. Nor further is it the case that the foundations of economic science have been found necessarily to be precarious, but rather that it is not at all clear precisely what they are. To this lack of fundamental clarity can be attributed to a certain extent the ferocious and interminable character of the many controversies that rage among economists themselves on the one hand, and on the other hand much of the uncertainty as to the significance of their results with which economists face the outside world.

Unfortunately, however, methodological writings and the discussion of *Grundprobleme* from every conceivable philosophical standpoint—Idealist, Materialist, Phenomenological, Transcendentalist, Neo-Kantian, etc., etc.—have, not unjustifiably, won a bad reputation among economic scientists. As Professor Schumpeter with particular reference to German conditions complains : [1] " Long enough have we searched after new paths, explored philosophical backgrounds, quarrelled over methods, represented and championed fundamental ' standpoints ' and ' positions ', and in general pursued economic theory as though it was philosophy, containing fundamentally different systems about which each has his own dogma ". In the less philosophically-minded Anglo-Saxon countries it is hardly surprising that many have turned their backs in impatience on " this noisy conflict of half-truths angrily denying one another ", and have abandoned the interminable wranglings and controversies of the " methodologists " and " philosophers " for seemingly more constructive work. But this evasion can only be temporary. For it can fairly be insisted that no advance in the elegance and comprehensiveness of the theoretical superstructure can make up for the vague and uncritical formulation of the basic concepts and postulates, and sooner or later—and at the moment it seems to be *sooner*—attention will have to return to the foundations.

What are the roots, then, and what is the way out of this dilemma of, on the one hand, the obvious pressing necessity for the critical clarification of the basic concepts and postulates, and on the other hand the interminable inconclusiveness of the controversies over the " methodological " and " philosophical " foundations ? A road must be found which leads definitively and conclusively forward and not simply round in a circle.

Of the literature on these problems it may be commented, first, that even to-day much of it appears to be concerned rather to attack or defend some particular " school ", or to lay down a " method " in the abstract, rather than with the detailed analysis and criticism of fundamental propositions in accordance with a definite criterion to which scientific propositions must attain. Here, as elsewhere, it is usually found easier when there is a lack of clarity about the particular to discourse on the general.[2] Secondly, as Professor Morgenstern recently pointed out,[3] the results of the

5

revolutionary developments in recent decades of the
science of Logic and logical analysis have scarcely
been made use of at all. Since Mill, Jevons, J. N. Keynes,
and W. E. Johnson, when Economics and Logic were
closely associated, there has been a division of scientific labour, and against the gains of increased
specialisation there may be losses to be set off.

But there is a far more important and fundamental
reason than either of these for the inconclusiveness
of the discussions of the " philosophical foundations
of Economics ", and that is the obscurity as to
whether the object in view is the " philosophical "
discussion of " philosophical " questions, or rather the
solution of " scientific " problems according to a
definite " scientific " criterion. These vague and highly
ambiguous adjectives " philosophical " and " scientific " are being used here in a sharply and clearly
separable sense and the distinction is of fundamental
importance for our discussion.

## 2. " SCIENTIFIC " AND " PHILOSOPHICAL " PROBLEMS

The scientist's activity may be described as the
taking over of the apparatus, results, and solutions
of his predecessors, the testing and, if necessary, the
rejecting of them according to agreed criteria, when
possible their improvement and development, and the
taking up of new problems—which he, in his turn,
passes on to his successors. It is reasonable to speak
of the " advance " of science owing to the possibility
of taking some results as, at any rate temporarily,
agreed upon and settled, and of then proceeding to
new problems and solutions. But one can scarcely
more appropriately speak of the *advance* of philosophy

from Plato to Hegel than one can of the advance of
poetry from Homer to Shakespeare, certainly not as
one can speak of the advance of Biology from Aristotle
to Mendel or even of Economics from Petty to
Marshall. The reason why scientists, unlike philosophers, can build on and advance their predecessors'
work rather than each being simply " influenced " by
it and starting afresh right from the beginning at the
same problems with some completely new system, is
that " scientists " have definite, agreed, and relatively
conclusive criteria for the testing of propositions,
solutions, and theories which " philosophers " do not
accept. It is this acceptance of the testing of propositions according to definite criteria which is the source
of that steady secular piecemeal agreement and
advance of " science ", and its cumulative, international, impersonal, and " coral-reef-like " growth.

This distinction between the " scientific " and
" philosophical " procedure may be developed by
means of a simple example.[4]

Two economists might have an argument as to
whether the cheque system did or did not exist in
Paraguay. They might be prepared to settle the dispute by referring to some book they accepted as
authoritative. But if there was no such book they
could themselves go to Paraguay and investigate, and
there is no reason to suppose that they would not soon
come to complete agreement as to whether, on their
definition of the terms, the " cheque system " existed
in " Paraguay " or not. Nor is there any difference in
principle if their argument did not relate to present-
day Paraguay but to Paraguay in the fifteenth century
before or after Christ, and if owing to the inconclusiveness and ambiguity of the evidence one economist

conjectured that " cheques " then did exist and the other that they did not. They could at any rate agree as to precisely what the evidence was, record that it gave rise to different interpretations, and that, failing the discovery of some new evidence, there was nothing else at all to be said. But supposing that the two economists had found that in present-day Paraguay the cheque system *did* exist, and actually had a cheque before them. Then, having settled the scientific dispute, they might begin a philosophical dispute. One of them might argue that they had not got the real cheque-an-sich before them, which was a transcendental cheque and for ever inaccessible, but only the idea or appear-ance of a cheque ; while the other might argue that, on the contrary, this printed slip of paper was the real essential cheque, and that ideas did not really exist, or that he did not know what a real cheque was, as the only ultimate reality for him was his own private subjective experience of seeing and touching a cheque and he had no idea whether someone else had the same real experiences or any experience at all. And so on. . . .

So long as the two economic scientists remained in their own scientific field their problem was one which could be brought to a definite test and ultimately settled one way or the other, and disagreement could thus in the end be removed. When, however, the two investigators went outside the scientific field, there was no such test. There was no agreed method of finding out whether their respective propositions were " true " or " false ", or of indicating what would have to be the case if one or the other was " true " or " false ", and there is therefore no reason to suppose that the disputants would necessarily ever come to agreement—as in fact in two thousand years philosophers never have. Further, if they *did* happen to agree it would be quite a different kind of " agreement " from that of two scientists who have accepted the result of an agreed test.[5] If such intersubjective tests could not satisfactorily be made, there could be no science. A world is quite conceivable in which they could not, just as no statistics or even agreed estimates can yet at any rate be obtained as to many social phenomena. It is simply an empirical fact that over large areas satisfactory agreement can be and is arrived at by such tests.

The scientist proceeds by means of the two inextricably interconnected activities of empirical investigation and logical analysis, the one, briefly, being concerned with the behaviour of facts, and the other with the language in which this is to be discussed. It is this latter activity as carried out in the science of Economics which it is largely the purpose of this book to analyse and itself to carry on. But if the finished propositions of a science, as against the accessory purely logical or mathematical propositions used in many sciences, including Economics, are to have any empirical content, as the finished propositions of all sciences except of Logic and Mathematics obviously must have,[6] then these propositions must *conceivably* be capable of empirical testing *or be reducible to such propositions* by logical or mathematical deduction. They need not, that is, actually be tested or even be *practically* capable of testing under present or future technical conditions or conditions of statistical investigation, nor is there any sense in talking of some kind of " absolute " test which will " finally " decide whether a proposition is " absolutely " true or false. But it must be possible to indicate intersubjectively what is the case if they are true or false : their truth or falsity, that is, must make some conceivable empirically noticeable difference, or some such difference must be directly deducible therefrom.

### 3. SCIENCE AND PSEUDO-SCIENCE

We suggest that the economic scientist is transgressing the frontiers of his subject whenever he resorts to, or advances as possessing some empirical content, propositions which, whatever emotional associations they may arouse, can never conceivably be brought to an intersubjective empirical test, and of which one can never conceivably say that they are confirmed or falsified, or which cannot be deduced from propositions of which that can conceivably be said. It makes no difference to such a transgression whether the proposition is an expression of ethical uplift or persuasion, political propaganda, poetic emotion, psychological " association ", or metaphysical " intuition " or speculation. If there is any object in pursuing an activity one calls " scientific ", and if the word " science " is not simply to be a comprehensive cloak for quackery, prejudice, and propaganda, then there must be a definite objective criterion for distinguishing propositions which may be material for science from those that are not, and there must be some effective barrier for excluding expressions of ethical or political passion, poetic emotion or metaphysical speculation from being mixed in with so-called " science ".

The most sinister phenomenon of recent decades for the true scientist, and indeed for Western civilisation as a whole, may be said to be the growth of

Pseudo-Sciences no longer confined to hole-and-corner cranks or passive popular superstitions, but organised in comprehensive militant and persecuting mass-creeds, attempting simply to justify crude prejudice and the lust for power. There is, however, one criterion by which the scientist can keep his results pure from the contamination of pseudo-science and there is one test with which he can always challenge the pseudo-scientist—a test which at once ensures precision and exposes the vague concepts and unsupported generalisations on which the pseudo-scientist always relies. As three scientists have insisted, who work in a field which is possibly in greater danger and in even greater need of a definite barrier against the rising tide of pseudo-science than is Economics : " The essence of science is the appeal to fact ".[7] This is an appeal which the scientist must always be ready and eager to see made, and where this appeal cannot conceivably be made there is no place for the scientist as such.

We have tried here very briefly to indicate the only principle or distinction practically adoptable which will keep science separate from pseudo-science, a principle in fact which, though only consciously and precisely formulated in recent years, has always more or less unconsciously been practised by scientists, and the employment of which in rejecting all propositions and concepts which do not fulfil it (e.g. the concept of " Absolute Space ") has been synchronous with the advance of science. To say that, in general, the natural sciences are less controversy-ridden, less split up into warring " schools " or " orthodox " and " unorthodox " parties, into " bourgeois ", " Nordic ", " Jewish ", and " workers' " sciences, and enjoy a greater area of common agreement, is simply to say that in general

11

this principle has, for various reasons, received earlier and fuller recognition here than in the social sciences —partly because, in the former, statistics and observations are at present on the whole technically easier to obtain, and partly because objective tests are more readily accepted since human passions and desires are not so closely involved in the former as in the latter.

We are not attempting here to exalt " scientific " propositions or problems above " non-scientific " ones. We do not argue that the meteorologist's " knowledge " of a sunset is either somehow superior or inferior to the poet's or artist's " knowledge ". Nor do we insist that this is *necessarily* exactly the most suitable defining line between these two planes of science and of non-science—though we prefer it to any other terminological suggestion we have seen.[8] We are simply concerned with a vitally necessary distinction, label it how one will. It is not the place here to argue for the adoption of this principle any further, or to render our brief formulation of it more precise. We leave this to specialist works on the Logic of Science and scientific method and on the tactics for the scientist to adopt against his intellectual enemies. Our object in this introduction is simply to indicate as shortly as possible the general attitude in which the particular problems of the succeeding chapters will be approached, and we believe that this will emerge sufficiently clearly. It is these particular scientific problems which are our concern rather than general methodological issues. We are not concerned so much to advocate a particular disciplinary principle or criterion for the scientist as to show what are the consequences for economic science when this principle that we suggest is followed out. In that sense the validity of our conclusions is independent of the question as to whether this principle is accepted. In Chapter V we shall be particularly concerned to apply it to the concepts of utility and social utility.

In the main this essay is addressed to economists who already broadly accept the criterion we propose, though not necessarily the precise wording of this sketchy formulation of it, and who are prepared to see it applied rigidly and unwaveringly to the particular concepts and postulates of theoretical Economics, not simply out of an aesthetic pleasure in rigour for its own sake, but for the highly practical and important reason that only through this principle have we at once a method of reaching agreement and a barrier against the pseudo-scientist. We therefore decline debate with those who do not hold with this criterion just as we should refuse to play chess with someone with whom we could not agree as to the rules, and we say with Pareto, who among economists seems to have been one of the first and most emphatic to insist on our principle : " Throughout the course of these pages, we are in the logico-experimental field. I intend to remain absolutely in that field and refuse to depart from it under any inducement whatsoever. If, therefore, the reader desires a judge other than objective experience, he should stop reading this book, just as he would refrain from proceeding with a case before a court to which he objected. If people who are disposed to argue the propositions mentioned desire a judge other than objective experience, they will do well to declare exactly what their judge is to be, and if possible (it seldom is) to make themselves very clear on the point." [9]

There are certainly writers on Economics who are

not prepared to accept this criterion and the discipline it implies. Professor Sombart, for example, makes a distinction between what he calls the method of Natural science and the method of Moral science (*Geisteswissenschaft*). Although this distinction derives originally from Mill's distinction between Natural and Moral sciences, by English writers it never appears to have been regarded as much more than a useful classification, significant particularly, perhaps, with regard to the different possibilities of prognosis in the two types of sciences. In most of the English standard works on Logic and Scientific Method, although a number of them have been written by authorities who had a particular interest in and understanding of the problems of the social sciences—for example, Jevons' *Principles of Science* and Johnson's *Logic*—the idea of some fundamental difference in method and criteria is not mentioned ; or else the contrary is obviously implied, that there is but one scientific procedure— that applied with most success up till now in the natural sciences, as, for example, the quotation from Mill at the head of this chapter says. Bentham also, perhaps the greatest English pioneer in social science, is exceedingly explicit on this point. But in Germany the doctrine that the social or moral sciences have quite other criteria and methods than the natural sciences, employing philosophical and artistic elements, is dominant to the point of orthodoxy, and the criterion we have proposed here for economic scientists would almost certainly be called " naturalistic " and inadequate for a social science. The " naturalistic " conception is at any rate very explicitly rejected by Professor Sombart. We do not want to argue over such a rejection, as this controversy over the *naturwissen-*

*schaftliche* and *geisteswissenschaftliche* methods is just one of those interminable and inconclusive controversies which never trouble the practical scientist faced with a particular concrete problem and which we want to keep clear of in this book. We may, however, indicate one or two of Professor Sombart's conclusions, as the contrast may make our own more clear.[10]

He is perfectly clear that in rejecting the criteria and method of " natural science " in order to include philosophical and poetical elements and the knowledge of " essences " (*Wesenserkenntnis*) he is giving up the prospect of the progress of the " moral " sciences and of their being of much practical use or applicability. They are to be " a luxury ", " tragically torn between science, philosophy, and art ". Unlike, however, the natural sciences, they are to press on to an " understanding " of the " essence " of things. (It is significant that there is no English technical term for the German *verstehen* here.)[11] Against those who deliberately choose this path with a clear knowledge of the consequences we have no objection to make—*atque idem jungat volpes et mulgeat hircos*. It is permissible to enquire, however, of those who thus reject the criterion we advocate as to what definite procedure they have for ever reaching agreement on any conclusion and whether they possess any intersubjective criterion for raising their so-called scientific (*geisteswissenschaftliche*) propositions above any sort of quackery and propaganda. It may further be remarked that it may not, possibly, be entirely a coincidence that precisely those academic circles in Europe which have most traditionally and conclusively rejected our " naturalistic " scientific criterion as unsuited for the moral or social sciences which are to aim higher at "understanding" the "essence" of the phenomena they deal with, have found themselves most powerless against the ravings of Pseudo-science and have even in a few cases positively facilitated or assisted its growth. Here at least there seem to be traces of an unholy alliance of undisciplined metaphysical yearnings with propagandist Pseudo-science, of the longing for the infinite with the will to power, a combination so typical of a certain philosophical direction.

### 4. THE SCOPE AND PROGRAMME OF THIS ESSAY

Sciences never begin with problems which come logically first—if they did they would probably make very slow progress—but they start at a "common-sense" level and have to build *upwards* their structure of laws and relations, and *downwards* their foundations —the latter task being by criticism and analysis to test and make precise the common-sense notions they start with, and to assure a logically firm and secure basis for the superstructure.[12] If one cares to call this latter activity—of which Einstein's criticism and revision of the fundamental concepts of Physics is an obvious example—"philosophical" or "methodological", as against the "scientific" work on the superstructure of science, one may. We do not regard this terminology as useful, however, for the "philosopher" and "methodologist" of a science, if his work is to be of use to the scientist as such, must accept and discipline himself to exactly the same criteria of empirical testability and logical consistency as the "scientific" worker on the superstructure.

Nor further can any clear line be drawn between

the problems of the infra-common-sense foundations and the supra-common-sense superstructure—the two are inextricably interconnected—and only the most complete confusion can ensue when those who do not accept the criteria of the scientist try and solve the basic problems of his science for him. It is sometimes argued that there are metaphysical assumptions underlying all sciences which the self-conscious and profound scientist must work back to and formulate, or that no science is safer than the metaphysical assumptions on which it rests. Actually we happen to believe that this notion of " metaphysical assumptions " has been shown to be completely misconceived. But even if this were not so—*posito non concesso*—we should urge that the metaphysical discussion should be kept strictly separate from the scientific, which should be pushed back as far as it could according to its own methods and criteria.

To be of use to the scientist the " methodological " problems must be worked out in closest co-operation with the scientific worker at the more advanced stage of the scientific structure of production and, within the limits implied in the scientific criteria, solely with an eye to his problems. The discussion of " methodological " questions—for the scientist at any rate—only has sense in connection with the practical problems of science.[13] Of course any economic scientist or " methodologist " will almost certainly save himself much thinking, many mistakes, and possibly his going completely off the rails, by making the fullest use of the modern works of specialists in Logic and the Logic of Science, who accept the same criteria as himself ; but the critical analysis of the basic concepts of economic science must be carried through to the end within the science itself and according to the scientific criteria, not according to the criteria of outside philosophers.

To the objection of a rather Anglo-Saxon type that it is better to settle the problems of the basic concepts by "sound instinct and common sense" without entering into "philosophical refinements" (to which attitude that of business men and popular newspapers to economic theory may be compared), it would be answered that it is precisely the task of science to supersede crude common-sense notions by critical analysis, and further that it is the unsatisfactory state of the foundations beneath the common-sense surface which is the most serious and crippling deficiency of contemporary economic science, since other deficiencies lie rather in the nature of the subject matter as compared with that of natural sciences and may never be thoroughly overcome in the same way.[14]

In concluding this introductory chapter we wish to emphasise once again that this book is concerned to seek solutions of certain basic problems of economic science in accordance with the criteria we have here outlined. It is not concerned to urge or to appear to urge any ultimate "necessity" or "absoluteness" about these criteria, although, not attempting to hide our personal intellectual tastes, we have tried to indicate here some consequences of their adoption on the one hand and their rejection on the other.

## NOTES

1. Cf. J. Schumpeter, Introduction to E. Barone's *Grundzüge der theoretischen Nationalökonomie*, p. 7.

2. Cf. J. Schumpeter, *Wesen und Hauptinhalt der theoretischen Nationalökonomie*, p. xiii: "In allgemeinen methodologischen

Werken ist von konkreten Problemen meist gar nicht die Rede ; vielmehr bewegt sich die Diskussion in allgemeinen Behauptungen ".

3. Cf. O. Morgenstern, *Zeitschrift für Nationalökonomie*, 1936, p. 1.

4. Cf. R. Carnap's essay, *Scheinprobleme in der Philosophie*.

5. Cf. J. Schumpeter, *op. cit.* p. 24 : " Aber müssen wir wirklich warten bis sich die Menschheit über diese Fragen klar geworden ist ? In diesem Falle müsste man die Ökonomie überhaupt aufgeben, da manche derselben sicherlich erst mit dem letzten Atemzuge des letzten Menschen verstummen werden."

6. This seems to us obvious. But the contrary view that Economics is, or ought to be, not an empirical science at all but a formal science just like Mathematics and Logic is held by a number of authorities led by Professor L. von Mises. Cf. *Grundprobleme der Nationalökonomie* and his lecture in *Actes du Congr s International de Philosophie*, Paris, 1937. In future references we may, for reasons of brevity, omit this obvious qualification to the Principle of Testability : that a scientific proposition may not itself be empirically testable *directly*, but may be reducible by direct deduction to an empirically testable proposition or propositions (cf. propositions of Physics about electrons, $\alpha$ and $\beta$ particles, etc.).

7. Cf. J. Huxley, A. C. Haddon, and A. M. Carr-Saunders, *We Europeans : A Survey of " Racial " Problems*, p. 287.

8. We prefer this terminology—" science " and " non-science " —for the distinction, to that of " sense " and " nonsense " which used to be employed by writers of the former Vienna circle. To speak, however, of " scientific " propositions may well be misleading if it is not clear that all that is meant is that they might *conceivably* be recognised as scientifically " true ", not that they necessarily are so. The most fantastic proposition—*e.g.* the National Income of England is £1 per annum—might *conceivably* be material for science since it is empirically testable by statistical investigation.

9. Cf. V. Pareto, *The Mind and Society*, p. 14, and *Manuel d'Économie Politique*, p. 28.

10. Cf. W. Sombart, *Die Drei Nationalökonomien*, pp. 337-42 : " Deshalb kann man auch mit gutem Fug in den Naturwissenschaften von einem ' Fortschritt ' reden. Dass das Wissen kein Wesenswissen sondern nur ein Regelwissen ist, macht diesen ' Fortschritt ' möglich. Die Geisteswissenschaften können dieses Ideal schon deshalb nicht haben . . . da zu dem blossen Sachwissen

noch andere Bestandteile hinzutreten : just philosophische und künstleriche, so dass jedes vollkommene Erzeugnis geisteswissenschaftlichen Schaffens sich uns immer auch als ein philosophisches und Kunstwerk darstellt. . . . In dieser unausgesetzten Spannung zwischen den Anforderungen der Wissenschaft und der Verlorenheit an Philosophie und Kunst tritt das innerste Wesen der Geisteswissenschaften zutage, liegt aber auch ihre Tragik begründet. . . . Sie sind ein Luxus im wahrsten Sinne des Wortes."

11. Among writers on Economics, Gottl and Spann, in addition to Sombart, have particularly devoted themselves to the theory of *verstehen* without, for the non-philosophical reader, coming to any very clear or agreed results. What is common to all these writers appears to be a certain contempt for the natural sciences, and a wish to detract from the authority they enjoy and to obtain more respect for their own activities by explaining that the natural scientist never " understands " the " essence " of what he studies. We agree with Professor Sombart that Spann is right in calling his work Economic Philosophy and not Economic Science.

12. Cf. B. Russell, *Introduction to Mathematical Philosophy*, p. 2.

13. Cf. J. Schumpeter, *op. cit.* p. 7.

14. Cf. M. Weber, *Gesammelte Aufsätze zur Wissenschaftslehre*, p. 206.

## II

## THE PROPOSITIONS OF PURE THEORY

1. " *Die neuere Methodenlehre unseres Faches bietet in dieser Hinsicht ein trauriges Bild : Man redet fortwährend von Theorie, ohne ihren logischen Charakter auch nur im mindesten erfasst zu haben.*"
W. EUCKEN
Kapitaltheoretische Untersuchungen, 1934

2. " *Literary economists . . . are to this day dilly-dallying with speculations such as ' What is value ? ' They cannot get it into their heads that things are everything and words nothing, and that they may apply the terms ' value ' and ' capital ' to any blessed things they please, if only they be kind enough—they never are—to tell one precisely what those things are.*"
V. PARETO
The Mind and Society

3. " *Economists are quite unable to keep questions of language separate from questions of fact, and frequently have long arguments about words in the belief that they are making discoveries about the economic system.*"
Basic English for Economics

4. " *Insofern sich die Sätze der Mathematik auf die*
21

*Wirklichkeit beziehen, sind sie nicht sicher, und insofern sie sicher sind, beziehen sie sich nicht auf die Wirklichkeit.''* A. EINSTEIN
Geometrie und Erfahrung

# II

## THE PROPOSITIONS OF PURE THEORY

### 1. PROPOSITIONS OF PURE THEORY

THE term " pure theory " is one commonly and rather loosely used by economists, but for the purposes of more precise analysis it is better replaced by the concept of the *type of proposition* of which " pure theory " consists.

By a " proposition of pure theory ", then, we understand one of the form " Under perfect competition firms are of optimum size ", or " With an increase in M, and with V and T remaining the same, P rises ", or " If p then q ", or " $p \supset q$ ".

Propositions of pure theory, on our definition, are to be sharply marked off from two other types of proposition. They are to be distinguished, *first*, from propositions of the form " Conditions of perfect competition hold in this or that market, therefore firms are of optimum size ", or " M has risen and V and T have remained the same, therefore P has risen ", or " *Since* p *therefore* q ". These might suitably be called " propositions of *applied* theory ".

In this latter type of proposition the premise " p " is asserted as true empirically, while in " propositions of pure theory " no empirical assertion as to the truth of p or q individually is made. The statement made is that of a certain relation between the premise

23

p and the conclusion q. "*Since* p *therefore* q " is equivalent to two propositions, (1) the proposition of pure theory " If p then q ", and (2) the empirical synthetic proposition " p is true " (and, if one likes, thirdly, the further assertion as true of the empirical synthetic proposition q). An adequate symbolism makes the distinction between the proposition of pure theory, p ⊃ q and ⊢ p. p ⊃ q, perfectly clear,[1] and shows that the latter consists of two quite separate propositions either of which may be " true " individually while the other is " false ".

We have been assuming that the premise " p " is an empirical synthetic proposition. For the particular distinction we are here drawing it makes no difference if " p " is an analytical proposition or a definition, for example, " All economic conduct is *ex definitione* rational ". The obviously fundamental distinction in the significance of " If p then q " when " p " is a definition, and " If p then q " when " p " is an empirical synthetic proposition, will be examined later.

The " truth " or " consistency ", then, of " propositions of pure theory " is quite independent of the question of fact as to whether the premise (of course when it is an empirical synthetic proposition) is empirically true or not, though it is on this question of fact that its applicability depends.[2] In this sense, propositions of pure theory are independent of all facts, which can be of any conceivable kind without their *consistency* being affected. We may compare a proposition of pure theory with the empirical assertion of the truth of a premise to the following distinction between a proposition of pure geometry and a proposition of applied geometry : " Thus a geometrical principle, when applied to a concrete presented object,

24

is *a priori* and certain in the form ' If this plot of ground is triangular and our space is Euclidean, then the sum of these angles is 180 degrees '. But when the hypothesis is dropped and we assert ' The sum of these angles is 180 degrees ', the judgment is probable only, because there is no *a priori* and complete assurance that the concept ' Euclidean triangle ' is genuinely applicable to this plot ".[3] As Jevons put it : " If a triangle be right-angled the square on the hypotenuse will undoubtedly equal the sum of the squares on the other two sides ; but I can never be sure that a triangle is right-angled ".[4]

These quotations bring us to the second type of proposition from which propositions of pure theory must be sharply distinguished, that is, from propositions like " If the clouds are grey it is going to rain ", or " If you offer a man unconditionally *either* one shilling *or* one pound he will take the pound ", or " If one has only seven loaves and a few little fishes, one cannot feed and satisfy four thousand hungry people ". For this type of proposition we may invent the symbol p s q.

It is a defect of ordinary language that there is not necessarily any distinction, as regards the outward form, between p ⊃ q, a deductive inference, and p s q an inductive inference.[5] The latter does not signify any logically " necessary " relation between p and q but a *conceivably* falsifiable, even if *in fact* not falsified inductive generalisation, the falsification of which, however miraculous and absolutely unprecedented, is nevertheless conceivable, and the negation of which produces no contradiction in terms. In loose every-day language a proposition may be ambiguous as between the two types. For example, before the dis-

covery of black swans in Australia the proposition
" All swans are white " might have been defined as
an inductive generalisation conceivably falsifiable, or
as a definition that creatures that were not white
were not to be called " swans ". But these are obviously quite as much two different propositions as
the propositions " This is a dear 'house " when it is
equivalent to " This is a charming house ", and " This
is a dear house " when it is equivalent to " This is an
expensive house ", and equally in both cases any one
who understands what he is talking about must be
able to indicate which he means. But whereas, with
the former type of ambiguity, a house may be both
charming and expensive without a contradiction in
terms, a proposition cannot *both* be conceivably falsifiable by empirical observation, and *not* be thus conceivably falsifiable.

This, it is perhaps necessary to emphasise, is a
matter of deliberate definition. We propose this as a
" division by dichotomy ", as it is called, or exhaustive
twofold classification of all propositions which have
" scientific " sense. According to our definitions of the
terms—and we suggest that they are quite normal and
straightforward—either a proposition which has sense
is conceivably falsifiable by empirical observation or
it is not. If it is not thus falsifiable it does not, if true,
*forbid* any conceivable occurrence, but only a contradiction in terms. Propositions obtain their empirical
content simply in so far as, if true, they *exclude*,
*restrict*, or *forbid* something (*e.g.* " This table is
wooden ", if true, *forbids* or *excludes* " This table is
of iron ", etc.). Therefore a proposition with empirical
content or an empirical proposition must, by definition, be conceivably falsifiable, that is, if true, *exclude*

some conceivable possibility. Conversely, a proposition with sense, the validity of which does not depend on any empirical observation, cannot, by definition, exclude any conceivable possibility, and is therefore devoid of empirical content. The price of the unconditional necessity and certainty of propositions of pure logic and mathematics (and of propositions of pure theory) is, therefore, complete lack of empirical content.[6] According to our proposed definition all propositions with scientific sense, then, are either conceivably falsifiable by empirical observation or not, and none can be both.

It has been necessary to analyse this classification in such detail because it has been argued that those who adopt it " deny the existence " of some conceivable type or types of proposition. We make no such empirical proposition, but simply propose a classification which cannot be " true " or " false " but simply convenient or inconvenient. We suggest that, at any rate for the purposes of the economic scientist, it is the most obviously convenient classification,[7] and we propose to make use of it for this essay.

## 2. THE " NECESSITY " OF PROPOSITIONS OF PURE THEORY

Before pursuing our logical analysis any further we may turn aside for a moment to an inductive confirmation that it is leading us in the right direction. It seems to have escaped emphasis that throughout the history of economic theory there is a persistent record of accusations and counter-accusations of " circularity " and " assuming what one requires to prove ". Hardly any of the well-known theories of economists

27

from the Physiocrats onwards have escaped such a characterisation at one time or another.[8] In recent years the term " tautology " came to be applied, apparently with a derogatory innuendo (usually " a sheer ", " a mere ", or " no more than a " tautology), to various propositions of deductive theory, for example the Quantity Theory of Money and different variations of it in terms of saving and investment, the marginal productivity theory of interest, and other propositions.

It was not quite clear what was meant by this terminology or what other form of proposition apart from " mere tautologies " it was intended to arrive at by the procedure of pure theory. Possibly the purely " subjective " psychological characteristic of " obviousness " or " self-evidence " was being confused with logical type. Because the proposition $2 \times 2 = 4$ is to most people probably obvious or " self-evident ", while the proposition $17 \times 37 = 629$ is probably not, this does not imply that they are of different logical type. Similarly, though the proposition " If there is an increase in M, and V and T remain the same, there will be a proportionate increase in P " is " obviously a tautology " recording a terminological agreement, the proposition " Under perfect competition firms are of optimum size ", though possibly at first not obviously so, possesses the same logical character. Though certainly it would be fantastic to deduce a fact about the nature of the costs of a firm from a purely geometrical argument, this is not what has been done in this latter proposition. No empirical proposition recording a fact about costs has been stated; attention has been called, simply, to the relations between definitions—a " fact " of linguistic usage if one likes.[9]

If necessary, we can follow out the deduction of this proposition in detail. We start from the assumption, first, that the firms act " sensibly ". This is defined as balancing marginal cost against marginal revenue—or to include that—an, in a certain degree, arbitrary procedure, because there are many alternative definitions of " sensible " that might be given under which we could *not* say that sensible firms balanced marginal cost against marginal revenue. But obviously, rather than go through this process of definition we might have started with this as our initial assumption—that the firms balance marginal cost against marginal revenue. Similarly with the second assumption, which is " equilibrium ". This term is defined, as applied to the firm, as having average cost equal to price. We might, then, here also have started with this as an initial assumption. The third assumption is " perfect competition ". In ordinary life these words might mean all sorts of things. But in Economics, though originally it was arbitrary, the accepted definition of the term is " conditions such that the demand, or average revenue curve, for the individual firm is perfectly elastic ". As we are accepting this conventional definition we might have made it one of our initial assumptions. But this, by definition (and in no other way), implies that marginal revenue equals price. It appears, then, that in a sense, instead of going through this arbitrary process of assigning definitions, we might have started straight off by saying, " Let us assume marginal cost is equal to marginal revenue, is equal to price, is equal to average cost ". Here we may fit in the now accepted, but originally arbitrary, definitions of the terms marginal and average cost. These are such that they can only be equal when average cost is at a minimum. Again, we might have started with this as our one assumption. But there is now a recognised definition for " working at minimum average cost "—that is, " being of optimum size ". Our conclusion was thus assumed when we made our assumptions, and was reached by assigning definitions.

If we assume these assumptions and definitions our conclusion is already assumed—the proof is the process of recognising what we have assumed in our definitions. " Propositions which form part of logic, or *which can be proved by logic*, are all tautologies. . . . Such propositions, therefore, are really concerned with symbols, because they are only concerned with symbolic manipulations." [10]

In formulating a system of definitions one is in one and the same process formulating a series of analytical-tautological propositions of pure theory. Unless one is prepared to contradict oneself—that is, use language inconsistently by defining a concept in one way and then using it in another—once one has formulated a system of definitions one must agree to the resulting propositions of pure theory. Purely theoretical analysis consists in the manipulation of concepts in accordance with the rules laid down in their definitions. The assigning of definitions, therefore, obviously plays a key rôle in the construction of pure theory.

The selection of good definitions which make possible the development of useful deductive chains is indisputably a creative scientific achievement, but the selection of a definition does not involve an issue of truth or falsity in the same sense that an empirical synthetic proposition is either true or false.[11] A definition may be misleading, inappropriate, or inconvenient, and if a scientist prefers using one definition or system of definitions to another there is no way of ultimately confuting him so long, of course, as he uses them consistently. In this sense, though the use of this adjective seems sometimes to encounter resistance, definitions are "arbitrary".[12] The convenience or inconvenience of a definition will turn mainly on the actual facts to which it is to be applied, in Economics on what statistics may or may not be available.

Whether in introducing a new term altering, sharpening, or confirming the sense of an old one, a definition lays down a convention made by the scientist, who imposes it as a government does a traffic regulation. It is this law-giving element in the assignment of definitions which is the source of the "necessity" or "inevitability" so often claimed for propositions of pure theory, which at bottom are necessary and inevitable because we make them so—the reverse of what is the case with empirical generalisations, which, in a sense, are imposed on us by the behaviour of the facts.

Although theoretical economists have sometimes emphasised that they are aware that propositions of pure theory are concerned with definitions, not with facts, nevertheless in Economics, as apparently in Philosophy, Mathematics, and other sciences, countless controversies and confusions have resulted from the use of the "material" rather than the "formal" mode of expression.[13] Take, for example, propositions such as "Value *is* this", "Costs *really are* this", "No, they are that",[14] "What *is* saving or capital or the stationary state?" The form of these propositions leads one to the misleading notion that one is treating of something other than a question of language—put crudely, that one is talking about things and not about words. It appears that these propositions must be definitely right or wrong, and that there must be one correct answer to the questions. But when they are expressed in the accurate "*formal*" mode, for example, " In the Marxian language-system value is defined as follows . . .", or " I propose that in the language-system (economic theory) which economists are constructing the word 'saving' be defined as follows . . .", it is clear at once that the issue is fundamentally one of convenience, of how the definition fits in with others in the language, and is not one of absolute rightness or wrongness. When the relativity of a proposition such as " Perfect competition is, etc. . . ." to a particular language-system is admitted, and placed in the foreground from the start, there is more chance of profitable discussion and less of beating the air.

It would be completely fallacious to conclude that because we have insisted that various disputes — in fact *all purely theoretical* disputes which do not turn on questions of fact—are purely *verbal*, that therefore we are necessarily saying that they are *trivial*. On the contrary, it is arguable that, particularly with regard to the theory of the trade cycle, for example, attention to the question of arriving at an accepted and unified system of definitions would be amply rewarded, instead of continuing with each writer having his own private terminology and imagining that he has found out something new about the trade cycle—some " Fundamental Relation " or other—when he has simply added to the already vastly excessive number of terminologies. But constructive verbal discussion can only begin when it is perfectly clear that it is verbal and purely verbal.

Similarly when we, or quotations we have cited,

have spoken of propositions of pure theory as " simply "
or " only " concerned with symbolic or terminological
manipulations, we are, of course, not trying to level
a deliberate insult at propositions of pure theory or
those who work at them, and to scorn them as being
concerned simply with trivialities. But it is the feeling
that important scientific work is being somehow be-
littled and analysed out of existence which seems often
to be behind the resistance to such analysis as this,
when no alternative logico-scientific analysis of analytical propositions devoid of unscientific mysticism
is put forward.

### 3. THE USE AND SIGNIFICANCE OF PROPOSITIONS OF PURE THEORY

Let us turn from examining what we have called
propositions of pure theory from the point of view of
*the source of their necessity* to an examination of *their
use and significance*. The rôle of analytical propositions
in science has been clearly summarised by Schlick as
follows :

" The construction of any strictly deductive science
is, as it were, a game with symbols. In an abstract
science like the theory of numbers, for example, it is
simply the enjoyment of this game for its own sake
which is the motive for the building of a deductive
structure. But in geometry, on the other hand, and to
an even greater extent in other sciences the interest
above all lies in certain other perceptual (*anschauliche*)
objects to which there is a possibility of linking the
net of concepts. In general, then, we concern ourselves
with the abstract only in order to apply the results to
the concrete. But in the moment of transferring a rela-

tion of concepts to perceptual examples the exact rigour is no longer preserved. For if any object is given us, how can we ever know with absolute certainty that they stand to one another in precisely those relations which are laid down in the postulates through which we define our concepts ? " [15]

Being unconditionally true and neither confirmable nor contradictable by an empirical synthetic proposition, propositions of pure theory cannot tell us anything new in the sense of telling us new facts about the world. But they call attention to implications of our definitions which might otherwise have escaped our attention, and reveal unexpected relations between our definitions which are thus explained and clarified.[16] " Pure theory " affords us a sharp clear-cut language or system of definitions with which to approach the problems which the facts of the world raise. Just as theoretical physicists and astronomers have the task of explaining everything we say by implication if we assert the law of gravitation,[17] so theoretical economists have the task of explaining what we say by implication if we assert the various assumptions of economic analysis.

Propositions of pure theory enable us, further, to pass at once from one empirical synthetic proposition to another. Just as the proposition of pure mathematics " $7 \times 17 = 119$ " enables me to pass at once from the empirical proposition " My bookcase contains 7 rows with 17 books in each row " to the further empirical proposition " My bookcase contains 119 books ", so the proposition of pure theory " Under perfect competition firms are of optimum size " enables one to pass at once from the proposition " Competition is perfect in this market " to the proposition " The firms competing in this market are of optimum size ". Their use thus depends on one's being able to establish an empirical proposition as true. In some kind of perfectly fluid world even mathematics would be inapplicable.

Theoretical analysis thus compensates us, in a certain way, for the fact that our brains are not all-powerful.[18] With all-powerful brains we would need no pure theory to work out the relations and implications of our definitions or empirical premisses. We would just have a dictionary in which all our concepts —" perfect competition ", " monopoly ", " saving ", etc.—were clearly defined and, after reading it through, would perceive at one glance all the most subtle inter-relations. As it is, pure theory, by consistent uncontradictory use of the economic vocabulary and by building up the vocabulary further, brings home to us what the implications of our definitions are.

A sharply and clearly defined system of concepts enables sharp and clear answers to be obtained from empirical investigation. The " man in the street " asks whether " wages " have risen since 1920, and getting four or five different answers, concludes that " one can prove anything by statistics ". This is quite a correct conclusion if one is proceeding without sharply defined concepts. An economist distinguishing between " money " wages and " real " wages, wages per hour and wages per month, can squeeze the maximum of definiteness and clarity out of the available statistics. The constant object of the scientist, it has been said, is to compel the facts of experience to answer his questions definitely " Yes " or " No ",[19] and he can only do this with a clear-cut language-system. As the classic advocate of induction admitted : *prudens interrogatio dimidium scientiae*—a half, but only a half, for, to quote Poincaré, " all that the scientist creates in a fact is the language in which he enunciates it ".

Every single step in a deductive chain is trivial. Long deductive chains lose their trivial, but not their analytical-tautological character. To criticise a proposition of pure theory *as such* as tautological, or circular, or as assuming what it requires to prove, is beside the point. The *applicability* of the assumptions of a piece of pure theory may be criticised; but this is purely a question of fact, having nothing to do with the *form* of a proposition of pure theory, which *must* necessarily be " tautological ", " circular ", and " assume what it proves "—for what it proves must be contained in the assumptions, and cannot be obtained from any other source. As Professor Lewis puts it : " The test of circularity is a valuable test of any deductive development of logic. That the principles proved are precisely the principles used in the demonstration of them is here a matter for congratulation. That the method of our proof coincides with the results of it, is a test of both method and result. It is not a test of truth, however, it is a test of formal or methodo logical consistency." [20]

#### 4. THE HYPOTHETICAL METHOD

To a far greater extent than any other science, except perhaps Geometry, Economics makes use of what has been called the " hypothetical " or " isolating " method. That is, much of the economist's work is devoted to investigating not directly the problems of the world as it is, but simplified cases and examples which, it is claimed, " throw light on the real problems ". Communities of perfect competition, with "neutral" money, communities in some sense "static" or " dynamic ", the behaviour of a Robinson Crusoe and other " conjectural history ", as Sir James Steuart called it, of every description is investigated.[21]

The same or a similar method was that called " the hypothetical experiment " by Cairnes.[22] As a modern writer puts it, " Economic theory is a laboratory for the economist " ; [23] or, to take a fuller description by Böhm-Bawerk : " Just as the experimenter artificially simplifies the conditions under which he tests the workings of certain forces or materials, and excludes the disturbing ' frictions ' of the world as it is, so the deductive, but by no means a *priori*, theorist isolates in this thought the workings of certain typical social or economic forces to examine them first free of disturbances in their purity, and out of the partial knowledge obtained in this way gradually pieces together his knowledge of the full and varied empirical reality. His simplified and simplifying premisses are in the same sense real as the contents of the experimenter's test-tube." [24]

It is clearly very necessary here, when it is claimed, apparently, that the simplified hypothetical " experiment " of the deductive theorist is a full substitute for the laboratory experiments of the natural scientist, to emphasise the distinction drawn at the beginning of the chapter between a proposition of pure theory— a *deductive* inference or logical implication—and an *inductive* inference won by experiential observation, for, in our imperfect everyday language, they may both be worded in the same way (" If p then q ").[25]

The result of an empirical experiment, however

isolated and artificial the conditions under which it is carried out, is recorded in a synthetic empirical proposition. It is always conceivable that if the experiment were repeated the result might be different, and either a generalisation based on previous similar experiments would be falsified, or some disturbing element or a " mistake " might be recorded.

It may perhaps be psychologically useful in some cases for an investigator to imagine and describe to himself the workings of some particular model community representing an extreme case. But this cannot be anything more than a preliminary thought-clearing exercise, and it would be fantastic to suggest that one could thus achieve the concrete results obtainable from laboratory experiment for which this procedure constitutes a substitute.

But the procedure of the so-called " hypothetical experiment " is completely different. Here certain simplifying assumptions are made, and then what we have called " propositions of pure theory " *without any empirical content*, are arrived at by pure deduction. When it is stated, for example, that static equilibrium analysis " examines in isolation part of the forces operating in the real world ", which tend to regain equilibrium like water in a tank when disturbed,[26] clearly there is a danger of propositions of the type $p \supset q$ being confused with propositions of the type $p s q$. Cairnes used, incidentally, for demonstrating a hypothetical experiment, that " mere tautology ", as it has been called, the Quantity Theory of Money, examining the " effects " on P of a rise in M when V and T remained the same.[27] This is one variety of many different kinds of attempts to read some empirical content into propositions of pure theory, to give them, as Professor Myrdal puts it, " einen scheinbaren Inhalt von Wirklichkeitserkenntnis ".[28] We discuss in the next chapter attempts to assign to them prognostic value, the statement of a causal connection, and, above all, their being called " laws ". Such attempts are no doubt partly due to this type of analysis usually being mainly carried on in the *material* rather than the strictly accurate *formal* mode of expression. The argument usually begins " We assume conditions of perfect competition . . ." or " Imagine a community . . .", instead of " The term ' perfect competition ' being defined as follows, it logically implies . . ."

The very terms " assume " and " assumption " may give a misleadingly " material " appearance to " purely theoretical " discussions, as though one was really considering an empirical possibility, by way of a model (as when in everyday language one says " Assuming it rains to-morrow "), and not simply analysing definitions.[29]

That " pure theory " is so often carried on in everyday language instead of the formal abstract language of mathematics may also give it a misleadingly " material " appearance, as the constant mention of markets, consumers, prices, goods, and so on inevitably calls up images in our minds which divert attention from the purely formal nature of the argument. It is necessary constantly to remember that " theories which make a proposition of logic appear substantial are always false ".[30]

In so far, then, as the propositions of hypothetical analysis are propositions of pure theory—that is, in so far as the assumptions on which they are based are not asserted as facts—to that extent hypothetical propositions say nothing about facts but about the way in which we discuss the facts. Hypothetical analysis or pure theory creates, as Ramsey put it, a " language for the discussing of the facts ".[31] All these relations between symbols say nothing about real experience ; they are but part of the instrument for mastering it. All these analyses of hypothetical simpli-fied communities—in so far as the resulting proposi-tions are of the form we have discussed (however mis-leadingly they may appear to be dealing with "things" and not " words " by beginning " Let us *assume* such-and-such *conditions* " or " Let us imagine a community where . . ., etc.")—are concerned with language. They are concerned in no way with some mystical " real " connection between facts which we discover by deductive thinking. Rather they have no direct connection with facts but flow from the way in which we talk about the facts.[32]

## 5. THE " CETERIS PARIBUS " ASSUMPTION

As an example of the use of the ceteris paribus assumption we may take the proposition " If the price at which a good is sold rises, ceteris paribus the amount of the good demanded declines ". Is this an empirical generalisation which can conceivably be false without any contradiction, or is it an analytical-tautological proposition ?

This, usually, is not made clear, and perhaps such propositions are sometimes meant in one way, some-times in another. One can only ask in each particular case whether the validity of the ceteris paribus pro-position in question depends on facts, or whether, on the other hand, the denial of it simply shows that one does not understand by the terms " rise in price " and " amount demanded " what the language of economists understands.[33]

If the proposition " If the price at which a good is sold rises, ceteris paribus the amount of the good demanded declines " is an empirical generalisation, so it can only have a clear scientific meaning if it is indicated under what conditions it would be true, or under what false. Further, it is desirable that the difference be shown between *this* empirical generalisation (*with* ceteris paribus) and the *other* empirical generalisation, " If the price at which a good is sold rises the amount of the good demanded declines " (*without* ceteris paribus).

Ceteris paribus propositions *can* be interpreted in this way. But if they are to be so interpreted—as empirical generalisations—then they are usually very vaguely and unclearly formulated. For no attempt is made, usually, to indicate under what conditions they are true and under what false, and the meaning of the vital qualification " ceteris paribus " is left hopelessly imprecise. The ceteris paribus assumption, just as much as any other, must be precisely formulated if the propositions it qualifies are to have any clear meaning. The *intention* of the assumption obviously is to lessen the falsifiability of the too often falsified generalisation " If the price of a good rises, the amount sold declines ". But exactly *how far* is its falsifiability thus lessened, and if it remains an empirical proposition, what conceivable possibilities of falsification remain ?

On the other hand, it seems more probable that ceteris paribus propositions are frequently treated as analytical-tautological propositions, the example taken in this case explaining a relation between the definitions of " rise in price " and " amount demanded " at different points on a demand curve of a particular shape—a purely logical or geometrical relation. Then it is inconceivable that its truth or falsity (as against its applicability) can be established by any facts, since it is without factual content. In this case one simply determines whether, in fact, the ceteris paribus assumption is true or false, by observing whether or not the price has risen appropriately or not—a circular procedure. This appears to be the interpretation favoured by Menger,[34] though it involves a very elastic conception of " *cetera* ". For example, if the well-known case of poor people buying *more* bread when the price of it rises in no way falsifies our proposition, this involves a considerable stretching of the assumption " ceteris paribus ".

Thus interpreted the ceteris paribus clause is an accessory assumption of pure theory, and ceteris paribus propositions may be analysed in the same way as the propositions of pure theory have been. The ceteris paribus assumption makes out of an empirical proposition that is concerned with facts, and therefore conceivably can be false, a necessary analytical-tautological proposition. For a mathematical solution (by tautological transformations) the number of equations must be equal to the number of unknowns. The ceteris paribus assumption sweeps all the unknowns together under one portmanteau assumption for a logical " solution ".

In Physics and Chemistry, where there are far more discovered empirical regularities, the ceteris paribus assumption is not used in the same way. For if the assumption is broadly true, or if, as is rather the case, the " *cetera* " in the natural sciences themselves act in accordance with known laws, then the ceteris

paribus assumption is more or less given one, and a
true premise can always be dropped. For in a certain sense it is only necessary to make an assumption
when one does not know it is true, or knows that it
is untrue. This is the peculiar dilemma — apparently unique throughout science—of the " isolating ",
" assumption-making " procedure of economic theory
where there are few empirical generalisations known
to be true.

In the natural sciences certain fundamental propositions can be taken either to be analytical-tautological or to be empirical generalisations, exactly as
the ceteris paribus propositions may be so taken.
For example, originally the proposition " All gases
expand on warming " was probably arrived at by
empirical experiments. But if to-day an experiment
was made with something which as regards the other
ways in which it was tested behaved like a " gas " but
did not expand on warming, one would at first be
inclined to suggest that some mistake had been made
in the experiment. But if after repeated experiments this " gas " did not expand, scientists would be
faced with a choice. Either they must say " Our
law that all gases expand on warming is destroyed,
and we must find a new law ", or they could say
" This stuff which does not expand on warming is no
' gas ', for *by definition* a ' gas ' *must* expand on warming ; we must find some other name for this ". The
choice of this second course on all conceivable occasions would mean that the proposition " All gases
expand on warming " was not an empirical law at all,
but an analytical-tautological definition which was
always true because it was not allowed to be false.
From the mere wording and form of the proposition

one cannot say whether it is the one or the other. One can only find out by a test case when scientists are forced to choose one alternative or the other.[35]

According to Edgeworth, " The treating as constant of what is variable is the source of most of the fallacies in Political Economy ",[36] and it is the danger of the ceteris paribus assumption that it particularly facilitates such fallacies. It is quite probably true that in more cases than not a rise in price is in fact followed by a decrease in demand, but this of course might not be so ; and whether it is so or not can only be decided by statistical investigation. Our proposition with ceteris paribus does not tell us this. In fact the ceteris paribus clause seems sometimes so to be used that one might equally significantly and correctly advance the proposition that ceteris paribus a rise in price is followed by an *increase* in demand, as the proposition that ceteris paribus it is followed by a *decrease*. " Ceteris paribus this follows that " seems to come to mean simply " *In many cases* this follows that ", and however often it may not, the reply is that the proposition only said " in many cases " (or ceteris paribus), and this was simply one of the other cases (or " ceteris paribus " did not hold).

In the recent developments of the " dynamic " pure theory of employment the ceteris paribus assumption appears sometimes to have been applied to propositions which standing alone (without " ceteris paribus ") are quite probably more often empirically false than true, but when it is added are meant to get away with some kind of exact and significant empirical content.

Mr. Keynes gives an example of the use of the ceteris paribus clause on these lines.[37] He contrasts the two propositions : (1) " A decreased readiness to spend . . . will ceteris paribus increase investment ", and (2) " A decreased readiness to spend . . . will ceteris paribus diminish employment ". Are these empirical or analytical propositions—that is, what is the precise content of " ceteris paribus " ? If they are empirical, then it is difficult to see what the qualification " ceteris paribus " can mean other than " usually ". Then we have two propositions : " A decreased readiness to spend will usually " either (1) " increase investment " or (2) " diminish employment "—two rather vague impressionist generalisations ; and though one *may* be more often true than the other, neither is of much scientific value compared with statistical investigations as to what, *in fact*, *does* follow a decreased readiness to spend in different cases, pending the results of which it seems difficult to justify an exclusive insistence on one as against the other.

If, on the other hand, these propositions are analytical, there is of course no question of one being " true " and the other " false ", and no particular reason for contrasting them, since neither says anything about *what in fact follows* a decreased readiness to spend. " Ceteris paribus " is simply used differently for the two equations. In the first *total outlay* is included among the " ceteris " that remain the same, so that a decrease in one division of it (consumption spending) mathematically implies an increase in the other division (investment). In the second equation *employment on capital goods* is assumed to remain the same, so that a decrease in employment on consumption goods mathematically implies a decrease in total employment.

Either of these interpretations is possible and there

45

may be others. In the first place such a use of the "ceteris paribus" clause leaves it quite ambiguous as to what kind of proposition is being put forward. In the second place it appears to give to what is either simply an empirically empty analytical proposition, or a very vague and statistically unsupported empirical generalisation, an air of some kind of precise and widely valid empirical content.

We suggest that the ceteris paribus assumption can only be safely and significantly used in conjunction with an empirical generalisation verified as true in a large percentage of cases but occasionally liable to exceptions of a clearly describable type.

## NOTES

1. Cf. L. S. Stebbing, *A Modern Introduction to Logic*, 2nd edition, p. 212.

2. F. Kaufmann, *Methodenlehre der Sozialwissenschaften*, pp. 38-57.

3. Cf. C. I. Lewis, *Mind and the World Order*, p. 313.

4. Cf. W. S. Jevons, *Principles of Science*, vol. i. p. 270. Also A. Einstein, *Geometrie und Erfahrung*, p. 3 ; J. Nicod, *La Géométrie et le monde sensible*, p. 14.

5. M. Schlick, *Allgemeine Erkenntnislehre*, 2, A, p. 43.

6. Cf. H. Feigl, *Theorie und Erfahrung in der Physik*, p. 11, and A. D. Ritchie, *Scientific Method*.

7. We emphasise very strongly that we are simply proposing a classification and not claiming that any conceivable type of proposition "does or does not exist". Neo-Kantian philosopher-economists may object that this classification is inconvenient as it passes over the Kantian synthetic propositions *a priori*, which cannot be fitted into it without distortion. We do not wish to go into the general philosophical or logical problems of Kantian criticism and exegesis on this point, though we happen to believe that all genuine problems here have been conclusively settled (cf. for example M. Schlick's *Allgemeine Erkenntnislehre*). We are concerned simply with a convenient classification *for economic scientists* and find that all the propositions of Economics

that we are concerned with in this book, including the Economic Principle (*vide* Chapter IV)—provided of course they are precisely and unambiguously formulated—at once fit into our classification. As regards the Economic or " maximum " principle it may be noted that Kant himself, it appears, would not have considered it a vastly significant proposition, and almost certainly not a synthetic one *a priori*, to judge by his comments on the concept of " Glückseligkeit ", *Kritik der Urteilskraft*, § 83 : " Der Mensch . . . ändert diesen (Begriff der Glückseligkeit) so oft, dass die Natur, wenn sie auch seiner Willkür gänzlich unterworfen wäre, doch schlechterdings kein bestimmtes allgemeines und festes Gesetz annehmen könnte, um mit diesem schwankenden Begriff, und so mit dem Zweck, den jeder sich willkürlicherweise vorsetzt, übereinzustimmen ". Cf. also the " neo-Kantian " T. H. Green's criticism of the Utilitarian principle : Introduction to Hume's *Treatise of Human Nature*, vol. ii. pp. 3-27.

If advocates of synthetic propositions *a priori* would agree and formulate—as they have not done yet, being content largely with generalisations—a number of these synthetic propositions *a priori* very precisely indeed, then we could begin to consider how they fit into our classification, which corresponds with that of most standard works on scientific method. An explanation would further be desirable as to how the " truth " of these propositions can be tested, if this cannot be done either by empirical verification or logical consistency, and whether or no they have empirical content and are conceivably falsifiable empirically. For the scientist just dogmatic assertion or question-begging phrases like " self-evidence " are hardly satisfactory. One neo-Kantian economist (cf. H. Bernadelli, *Economica*, 1936, p. 446 ; see also F. Kaufmann's apt reply, 1937, p. 337) admits that one is here led up against a brick wall, and concludes logically, but rather depressingly for the scientist, that as regards synthetic propositions *a priori* " so long as their source remains undiscovered all sciences which are built on philosophical or mathematical principles—and there is none which is not—hang so to speak in the air ". When one finds oneself in this position it may be better than insisting that the wall is not, or some day will not be, or ought not to be, there, to consider whether, possibly, one has not been on the wrong road from the start. A hopeless confusion over the term *a priori* in Economics also arises over its being somehow mixed up with " introspection " (*vide* below, V. 1-2).

8. See below, III. 1.

9. Cf. J. Robinson, *Economics of Imperfect Competition*, p. 95.

10. Cf. B. Russell, *Analysis of Matter*, p. 171, and R. M. Eaton, *Symbolism and Truth*, p. 227.

11. Cf. P. Frank, *Das Kausalgesetz und seine Grenzen*, p. 1.

12. Cf. L. Rougier, *La Structure des théories déductives*, p. 86 ; W. Dubislav, *Die Definition*, p. 112 ; and on the other hand, L. S. Stebbing, *op. cit.* p. 427 : " It is because definitions are not arbitrary that they are useful ". The disagreement is obviously an unimportant terminological one.

13. Cf. R. Carnap, *Logische Syntax der Sprache*, pp. 210 and 225, and *Philosophy and Logical Syntax*, pp. 46-81.

14. The " cost " controversy presents one of the most perfect examples of decades of argument over a purely verbal issue—though of course not necessarily the less important for that. Compare the following statement of the issues : " As is well known, Marshall and (up to a recent date) most of his followers insisted that costs, in the last analysis, were something real and absolute—a conception independent of utility. Wicksteed and the Austrians, on the other hand, denied that they were anything but foregone alternatives " (L. C. Robbins, Introduction to P. Wicksteed's *Commonsense of Political Economy*, p. xviii). Professor L. M. Fraser's *Economic Thought and Language* brings many such purely verbal controversies to light.

15. Cf. M. Schlick, *Allgemeine Erkenntnislehre*, p. 35.

16. Cf. A. J. Ayer, *Language, Truth, and Logic*, p. 104.

17. Cf. H. Hahn, *Logik, Mathematik, Naturerkennen*, p. 19.

18. Cf. R. M. Eaton, *General Logic*, p. 474.

19. Cf. K. Popper, *Logik der Forschung*, pp. 207-8.

20. Cf. C. I. Lewis, *Mind and the World Order*, p. 240.

21. W. Eucken, *Kapitaltheoretische Untersuchungen*, p. 7, clearly describes the hypothetical method and its importance : " Wenn ein isolierter Staat vorhanden, wenn das Land überall gleich fruchtbar ist, und wenn die übrigen von Thünen gesetzten Annahmen gegeben sind, dann muss der Standort der einzelnen Betriebssysteme sich da und dort befinden. Wenn ein Mann als Eremit lebt, wenn er bestimmte Bedürfnisse und ein bestimmtes technisches Wissen besitzt, wenn er über eine bestimmte Arbeitskraft verfügt und wenn noch mehrere andere Bedingungen gegeben sind, dann muss er auf bestimmte Weise bestimmte Produkte in bestimmter Menge herstellen. Der einzelne theoretische Satz enthält also ein hypothetisches allgemeingültiges Urteil über einen notwendigen Bedingungszusammenhang, *die moderne nationalökonomische Theorie als Ganzes stellt das in sich geschlossene einheitliche Gesamtsystem solcher Urteile dar.*" (Our italics.)

22. Cf. J. E. Cairnes, *Character and Logical Method of Political Economy*, 2nd edition, p. 90.

23. Cf. E. Phelps Brown, *The Framework of the Pricing System*, p. 32.

24. Cf. E. von Böhm-Bawerk, *Gesammelte Schriften*, p. 193, and also F. von Wieser, *Gesammelte Abhandlungen*, p. 19.

25. See above, Section 1.

26. See below, IV. 6.

27. Cf. J. E. Cairnes, *op. cit.* pp. 90-91.

28. Cf. G. Myrdal, *Beiträge zur Geldtheorie*, ed. F. A von Hayek, pp. 485-6.

29. In addition to the laboratory experiment and the so-called " hypothetical experiment " there is the *Gedankenexperiment*. This is simply letting one's fancy conceive what *might* happen if one tried some " real " laboratory experiment. *By itself* it yields no results at all ; it is simply the preliminary thinking-out of a possibly significant laboratory experiment and must always be followed up by that if it is to be proved valuable. Cf. E. Mach, *Erkenntnis und Irrtum*, ch. xi., and W. Dubislav, *Naturphilosophie*, pp. 60-62.

30. Cf. L. Wittgenstein, *Tractatus Logico-Philosophicus*, p. 155 ; J. Jörgensen, *Principles of Logic*, vol. iii. pp. 116-17, and L. Rougier, *op. cit., passim.*

31. Cf. F. P. Ramsey, *The Foundations of Mathematics*, p. 212.

32. Cf. H. Hahn, *op. cit.* p. 15.

33. Cf. K. Adjukiewicz, *Erkenntnis*, 1934, p. 263.

34. Cf. C. Menger, *Untersuchungen über die Methode*, pp. 57-9 : " Das Gesetz, dass der erhöhte Bedarf an einer Ware eine Steigerung der Preise, und zwar dass ein bestimmtes Mass der Steigerung des Bedarfes, auch eine ihrem Masse nach bestimmte Steigerung der Preise zur Folge habe, ist demnach, an der Wirklichkeit in ihrer vollen Komplikation geprüft, unwahr—unempirisch. Was beweist dies aber anders, als dass Ergebnisse der exakten Forschung an der Erfahrung im obigen Sinne eben nicht ihren Prüfstein finden ? *Das obige Gesetz ist trotz alledem wahr, durchaus wahr,* und von der höchsten Bedeutung für das theoretische Verständnis der Preiserscheinungen." (Our italics.)

35. Cf. K. Popper, *op. cit.* p. 230, and P. Frank, *op. cit.* pp. 241-50.

36. Quoted by O. Morgenstern, *Limits of Economics*, heading to ch. iii.

37. Cf. J. M. Keynes, *General Theory of Employment, Interest and Money*, p. 185.

# III

# THE APPLICATION OF PURE THEORY

1. " *One important lesson which the history of moral philosophy teaches is that, in this region, even powerful intellects are liable to acquiesce in tautologies of this kind, sometimes expanded into circular reasonings, sometimes hidden in the recesses of an obscure notion, often lying so near the surface that when once they have been exposed it is hard to understand how they could ever have presented themselves as important.*" H. SIDGWICK
Methods of Ethics

2. " *Votre Science est impeccable, mais elle ne peut le rester qu'en s'enfermant dans une tour d'ivoire et en s'interdisant tout rapport avec le monde extérieur. Il faudra bien qu'elle en sorte dès qu'elle voudra tenter la moindre application. . . . Le physicien ne peut demander à l'analyste de lui révéler une vérité nouvelle, tout au plus celui-ci pourrait-il l'aider à la présenter. . . . Toutes les lois sont donc tirées de l'expérience ; mais pour les énoncer, il faut une langue spéciale ; le langage ordinaire est trop pauvre, il est d'ailleurs trop vague, pour des rapports si délicats, si riches et si précis.*" HENRI POINCARÉ
La Valeur de la Science

**3.** " *Es ist nämlich recht merkwürdig zu beobachten :
die wissenschaftliche Richtung, zu der sich der
Verfasser dieser Arbeit nicht zählt, die abstrakte
Theorie mit sehr viel ambitiöseren Prätentionen
treibt, als nur möglichst klare und vollständige
Fragestellungen an die Empirie zu liefern, schafft
zuweilen eine Illusion von ' Realismus ', rationa-
lisiert in dem alten vernünftigen Gedanken, dass,
wie man zwei Beine zum Gehen braucht, man auch
in der Wissenschaft eine Zusammenarbeit von
' Deduktion ' und ' Induktion ' braucht. Allzu
oft muss die ' Induktion ' dabei aber bei ' praktischen Beispielen zur Beleuchtung des Gedanken-
ganges ' stecken bleiben, und damit ist man, oft
ohne es zu wissen, in dem theoretischen Absolu-
tismus, wo man auf ' deduktivem ' Wege allgemeine
Gesetze konstatiert, die man nachher mit ausge-
wählten Beispielen illustriert. Und im letzteren
liegt dann der ganze Realismus. Die Evidenz
ist systematisch selektiv.*"　　　 G. Myrdal

Beiträge zur Geldtheorie, (ed. Hayek)

# III

## THE APPLICATION OF PURE THEORY

### 1. THE SUBJECT MATTER OF ECONOMICS

WE are not concerned in this essay to attempt a definition of the subject matter of Economics. Though the discussions leading up to it may well be of interest, the actual assignment of a definition to the word "Economics" does not appear to solve, or even help in the solution of, any useful scientific problem whatsoever. The divisions between the individual sciences —the division, that is, of the scientific labour as a whole—have arisen more or less as the result of historical accident and considerations of convenience, and though scientists are rapidly becoming more self-conscious in their procedure, and though a " science of science " is growing up and it is interesting and suggestive to attempt to foresee what the most convenient division of labour is going to be, the laying-down of rigid frontier lines between the particular sciences seems an unprofitable undertaking leading to even more interminable disputes than those over national frontiers in Eastern Europe ; with the difference that whereas the ardent nationalists desire to *include* as much as possible, the definers of the subject matter of Economics seem often more concerned to turn out and *exclude* as much as possible. The suggested unprofitability of drawing hard-and-fast lines between the individual sciences is markedly in contrast with the desirability of drawing a simple and unambiguous line between " scientific " propositions that may be material used in some science or other, and propositions of metaphysics, poetry, political or ethical persuasion, which, though of course they can be studied " scientifically " and " scientific " propositions formulated about their occurrence, are not themselves " scientific " since they cannot conceivably ever be brought to any kind of empirical test.

We wish simply in this section to point out how certain authoritative definitions of its subject matter limit propositions of economic science to the type we called in the previous chapter " propositions of pure theory ".

A definition of the subject matter of Economics was given recently as follows : " The subject matter of Economics is essentially a series of relationships—relationships between ends conceived as the possible objectives of conduct on the one hand, and the technical and social environment on the other. Ends as such do not form part of this subject matter. Nor does the technical and social environment."[1] All facts, that is, are excluded, for technical, social, and psychological facts presumably comprise the entire possible factual material for the social scientist. Nor does Economics study economic conduct but begins just where the analysis of economic conduct leaves off, for this is " given " just as much as the social environment.[2] The task of the economist is pure deduction from selected postulates of what we have called " propositions of pure theory ", that is, propositions devoid of all empirical factual content and concerned solely with terminology.

What most scientists would regard as the problems they have to investigate, regularities in the facts of the world, are taken by the economist as assumptions, and he is said to venture outside his subject, to be concerning himself, as Pantaleoni put it, simply with " mere prolegomena or even digressions ",[3] or, to use Professor Strigl's phrase, only with " *Datenän-derungen* "—(changes in data—data being any empirical facts)—an " inexact " and even, one sometimes gets the impression, inferior activity, in an " irrational " field of study, in which other sciences can try their luck if they choose, but not the economist.[4] Certainly some of the writers call the subject they thus define " Pure " or " Theoretical " Economics, implying the possibility, apparently, of an untheoretical or impure Economics, though they seem to argue that this by itself can be an independent science. But in some cases—for example that quoted—it is " Economics " pure (very) and simple that is thus limited.[5]

Of course this definition, the object of which apparently is to guide economic studies in a particular direction, has not been arrived at out of the blue, but in fact, as its authors claim, simply makes precise the practice and the overt teaching of many of the classical writers of the science, brilliantly summed up in Ricardo's contrasting of " questions of science " with " questions of fact ".[6]

If the subject matter of Economics is defined in a way that excludes all propositions that are not analytical-tautological and " circular " in form, it is hardly surprising that every single central proposition and system of economic theory since the Physiocrats has, at some time or other, been criticised as circular, or as " assuming what it required to prove ".

After analysis of the central proposition of the Physiocrats, Professor Schumpeter writes : " No special doctrine remained except an analytical proposition in the Kantian sense that labour not applied to original production (*Urproduktion*) does not produce any new original product ".[7] Ricardo's theory of value was described by Bailey as saying no more than that what a million men produce by their work always costs the labour of a million men.[8] Of the Ricardian theory of rent Wicksteed held that it said nothing whatever but " that the better article commands an advanced price in proportion to its betterness ".[9] The wages fund theory is recognised as " resting on sound tautology ".[10] Cairnes said of Jevons' theory of value : " What does it really amount to ? In my apprehension to this and no more—that value depends upon utility, and that utility is whatever affects value. In other words, the name ' utility ' is given to the aggregate of unknown conditions which determine the phenomenon, and then the phenomenon is stated to depend upon what this name stands for. Suppose instead of utility we call the unknown conditions X, we might then say that value was determined by X ; and the proposition would be precisely as true, and so far as I can see as instructive as Mr. Jevons' doctrine. In either case the information conveyed would be that value was determined by the conditions which determine it." [11]

Passing to the Austrian theory of value as formulated particularly by Wieser, we find two American critics commenting upon its circularity.[12] The circularity of Professor Cassel's particular price theory has several times been pointed out, as also that of the Opportunity Cost theory,[13] while at one swoop Professor Mayer condemned all " functional " price theories, Cournot's, Jevons', Walras', Pareto's, and Cassel's, as " empty ", tautological, and circular.[14] As regards the marginal productivity theory of distribution, Marsha.. rather cautiously hinted at its circular reasoning and at its being a truism, " not a true theory ".[15] We do not wish to cite so " unorthodox " a writer as Veblen on the tautological character of Clark's theory of distribution.[16] In the field of monetary theory the Quantity Theory has long been recognised as " a mere tautology ", as have most of the more recent Fundamental Equations and Relations. It is surely superfluous to produce examples of such criticisms from the contemporary controversies over the theory of money and employment.

It must be remembered that when all these propositions were first put forward, it was claimed that they revealed what " determined ", " fixed ", or even " caused " or " measured " value, prices, wages, rent, and so on, and still to-day the discovery of what " determines " the level of employment, the rate of interest, or the course of the trade cycle is claimed in " circular " propositions of pure theory which, however valuable for an examination of the facts of economic life, the terminological precisions, clarifications, and proposals they may contain, are completely devoid of empirical content as to *causal* determination, and are concerned not with wages, employment, and interest at all, but with " wages ", " employment ", and " interest ".

## 2. THE LAWS OF ECONOMICS

The orthodox conception of the Laws of Economics corresponds closely with the conception of the subject matter discussed in the previous section, but is even more widely accepted.

Physiocratic Economics, according to Professor Schumpeter, was a member of the great family of the Natural Law system based on the *a priori* rationalist doctrines of the French and German philosophers of the eighteenth century. But if one omits the finalist element in their doctrines, " their conception of Laws as not simply the rules as to what in fact happens, but as something apart from the ' facts ', something to which men must submit in their actions . . . such Laws are precisely what without any contradiction are called the Laws of Economics to-day ".[17]

The " natural " laws of Ricardo and his followers, including notably Senior, were essentially of the same type. They were pure deductions based on not always pellucidly formulated postulates. These postulates described the " natural " community in a condition of perfect competition and with perfect or nearly perfect expectation—though this latter condition was not always made quite clear. The natural laws, that is, the " iron ", immutable, inexorable, and universal laws as they were sometimes described—subsequently to be called " static " or " normal " laws—were what we have called propositions of pure theory, strictly of a type with the proposition " Under perfect competition firms are of optimum size ".[18]

Menger contributed a further precision to this concept of economic laws, emphasising what he and subsequent writers called their *exactness*, exceptions to them being inconceivable, and that "it involved a misconception of the foundations and postulates of the exact method" to test them empirically.[19] The term "exact" apparently meant, simply, "arrived at by pure deduction", and there seemed a possibility that this term then, and subsequently, might be confused with the entirely separate empirical question as to the possibility of comparatively (not, of course, absolutely) exact *measurement* such as in the physical sciences. At any rate, the term "exact" lent an impression of strict scientific rigour to economic laws to take the place of the metaphysical and supernatural inexorability of the natural law conception, which the advance of the empirical method in the natural sciences had rendered quite untenable. To-day one can hardly help concurring with Schmoller that any worker in a chemical laboratory who proclaimed Menger's conception of exactness would be ejected forthwith.[20]

The influence of Menger's methodological writings on many contemporary economists of the Austrian direction has obviously been considerable. Economic laws are conceived of as necessary, exact, and unfalsifiable by empirical observation, deduced by pure logic from given postulates, as certain as the laws of Logic or Mathematics, and instead of the hidden hand of Adam Smith we have "the logic of the system" and "necessities to which human action is subject". Moreover it is only such propositions as these, "only those generalisations which have the character of certainty, which are Economic Generalisations proper".[21]

It is sufficiently clear that what are here called "economic laws" are what we have called proposi-

tions of pure theory, and—though the term " exact "
seems thoroughly misleading—we quite agree as to
their " necessity ". We should not, however, agree
that they possessed any empirical content or that they
said anything about the facts of the world. It is
difficult to avoid, however, almost complete agreement with Professor Sombart—however much one
may disagree with him on other issues—that the
impression one receives is that " the founders of the
theory of marginal utility and, it might be said,
almost all their followers, have seen in the laws they
propounded vast laws of nature . . . they have not
doubted that their laws contain information as to the
form events take ".[22]

Not only has it been insisted that what we have
called propositions of pure theory are the laws of economic science, but empirical laws such as—according
to the usual formulations—the law of diminishing
returns, Gresham's and Pareto's law, are obviously
regarded as inferior and unsatisfactory, and are
criticised for not being necessary, and even denied
the dignity of the term " law " altogether, it being
according to Pantaleoni " a misnomer to speak of
the economic law of decreasing productivity ".[23]
Either this, or, as Professor von Mises does for
Gresham's law, they are reformulated as " exact "
propositions of pure theory, and thus robbed of their
empirical content.[24]

Though the conception of laws that we have been
discussing appears from the Physiocrats down to the
present day to have dominated economic science,
this conception has been by no means exclusively
held. Jevons, at any rate in *The Principles of
Science*, and with great clarity Pareto [25] (though not

Walras), both conceived of economic laws in the same way that the chemist, biologist, or physicist to-day conceive of their laws. Marshall was obviously suspicious of the natural laws of the classics, but it is not absolutely easy to put one's finger on precisely the type of proposition which he regarded as stating economic laws. He begins with a perfectly clear description of the laws of economics as statements of what tends to happen, but then goes on to a discussion of their being " normal " laws (a term used by Cairnes as synonymous for " natural ") which abstract from disturbing frictions, and emphasises their long-run hypothetical character without drawing any distinction between deductive and inductive inferences.[26]

" A law ", as Mach put it, " consists always in a limitation of what is possible." [27] Economic laws of the orthodox type set no such limitation. They exclude or forbid no conceivable type of occurrence, being true, as their propounders insist, whatever happens or whatever might conceivably happen. They exclude simply the inconceivable, that is the contradictory—such as a figure being both round and square at once, or both eating one's cake and having it—where the definition of " eating cake " includes the definition of "ceasing to have cake". If one cared to change the usual terminology this would not be so, and it might be conceivably possible " to eat one's cake and have it "—similarly with the economic laws.

The emptiness of economic laws according to this conception emerges very clearly from Böhm-Bawerk's celebrated discussion of Power and Economic Law. The issue was shown to be not so much power *or* economic law as how power works itself out *within* economic laws.[28] " Everything called power goes into the data on which the laws hinge, so to speak." [29]

The economic laws, then, (unless of course particular assumptions are made and the whole question begged), do not show that " power " cannot and does not influence distribution, for they exclude no *conceivable* influence that " power " might exercise— if they did they would be conceivably falsifiable, which they are not allowed to be—and they would lose their iron and necessary character, and acquire empirical content.

But, it is frequently argued, every scientific law is necessarily " hypothetical ", in Economics as in all other sciences.[30] All scientific laws, it is insisted, begin with " if ". In a sense this is, of course, undeniable, but not in the vital and relevant sense. At the bottom of this argument lies the confusion noticed at the beginning of the previous chapter between inductive and deductive inferences.[31] By apparently all other scientists apart from logicians, mathematicians, and many economists, scientific laws are regarded as inductive, inferences *conceivably falsifiable*, though not *practically falsified*, empirically. If they are referred to as " hypothetical ", what is implied is rather their provisional falsifiable character, and that they may conceivably be abandoned at any moment. It would always be admitted that experiments might conceivably be made as to which it was agreed that there was no mistake or interfering factor, and of which the results were, say, that light and sound travelled at different speeds from those given in the accepted formulae. Though qualifying assumptions as to the conditions under which an experiment is to be carried out are introduced to lessen the falsifiability of a law, this falsifiability is not completely eliminated, as it is with the laws of Economics.

Another misconception as to economic laws appears to arise when it is argued that one and the same proposition can and does assert both types of law, empirical and deductive, at once, which are thus " synthetised " into one proposition.[32] Again, we may refer to the analysis of the previous chapter.[33] By definition either a proposition is conceivably falsifiable empirically or it is not, that is, either it has empirical content or it has not. Of course, one and the same *set of words* (" All conduct is rational " or " All swans are white ") can be interpreted in either of the two ways—just as any ambiguous word or set of words may have several interpretations, or just as " *couverts* " is usually to be interpreted as " knives and forks " in a French context and as " envelopes " in a German one. These are then two *different propositions* in the usual sense of this term—one can use another term if one likes. If all that is implied, however, is that the greatest terminological precision is required in reducing (but not eliminating) the falsifiability of empirical "laws", or that in the more advanced natural sciences many "laws" which started as empirical have been re-defined as analytical, then there is no disagreement.[34]

The conclusion of this section is that the prevailing tendency to call propositions of pure theory " laws " is misleading and inappropriate, and appears to be a survival from eighteenth-century rationalist philosophy and theology. A passage from an introductory work on scientific method seems very relevant to this misconception and the concept of science it implies, and we may quote it at some length : " If we attempted to describe science as a purely logical study in which propositions are deduced one from the other in a direct line of descent from simple ultimate assumptions to complex final conclusions, this double rôle of laws, partly assumptions and partly conclusions, would cause grave difficulty. All scientific arguments would appear ' circular ', that is to say they would assume what they pretended to prove. But the result that follows from our discussion is not that the science is fallacious, because it does not adhere to the strict rules of classical logic, but that those rules are not the only means of arriving at important truths. And it is essential to notice this result ; for since logic was the first branch of pure learning to be reduced to order and to be brought to something like its present position, there has been a tendency in discussion of other branches—and especially in discussion of science—to assume that, if they have any value and if they do really arrive at truth, it can only be because they conform to logical order and can be expressed by logical formulas." [35]

We suggest that the term " law " should be reserved only for those empirical generalisations such as Pareto's or Gresham's law or the law of diminishing returns, or diminishing marginal utility. It is such laws as these that it is the central object of science to discover. This is something more than the mere suggestion of a terminological change. It implies a fundamental alteration in the *quaesita* and methods of Economics. As has been well said : " The formulation of empirical laws is not just a special problem of the exact natural sciences but the central problem in the construction of all scientific theories, since empirical laws are the foundation for all scientific explanation ".[36]

## 3. PROGNOSIS AND CAUSALITY IN ECONOMICS

Just as one might say that the whole aim of science is the formulation of empirical laws, so it is only putting the same thing in another way to say that the aim of science is the formulation of prognoses. At any rate, any applicability or use for a science depends directly on the predictions it can make. We go then quite as far as Professor Knight when he says that " The aim of science is to predict the future for the purpose of making our conduct intelligent ".[37]

With regard to prognoses also, we find empirical content being read into propositions of pure theory just because of their necessity and inevitability. For example, it is sometimes argued that the very inevitability of economic analysis gives it great prognostic value, although economic science cannot at any time predict the data from which these inevitable implications are drawn.[38]

One might just as well argue: " It is this inevitability of the multiplication table which gives it its very considerable prognostic value. . . . The multiplication table knows no way of predicting out of the blue how long it will rain to-morrow, but given that it will rain for $10 \times 6$ minutes, it can draw the inevitable conclusion that it will rain for an hour." If, for example, the Quantity Theory of money could have been of use during the post-war currency inflations this would have been based on the inductive hypothesis or falsifiable prognosis that $V$ and $T$ would not vary sufficiently to counteract the

65

effect on P of a huge increase in M. That *given* a huge increase in M, and the constancy in V and T, there will be a huge increase in P, is as much a tautology devoid of empirical content as the Quantity Theory itself.

Not only is the high value emphasised of these " predictions "—which cannot conceivably be falsified, of course—but it is correspondingly insisted that no other kind of prediction is possible. For example : " The explanation of phenomena thus detected (by statistics) if it is to serve as a basis for forecasts of the future must in every case utilise other methods than statistically observed regularities ; and the observed phenomena will have to be deduced from the theoretical system independently of empirical detection ".[39]

The impression one inevitably receives is that because of its deductive apparatus Economics is in a position to make sure prognoses which are quite impossible in the other social sciences, and that prognosis depends on deduction and must be independent of " empirical detection ". This view was very explicitly stated by Robert Lowe : " In love, or war, or politics, or religion, or morals, it is impossible to foretell how men will act, and therefore it is impossible to reason deductively " ; whereas, " in matters connected with wealth, deviations arising from other causes than the desire of it may be neglected without perceptible error ".[40] Actually many predictions can be made in other social sciences quite as accurately and safely as any economic predictions, if not more so. The number of suicides or murders, or the population of London, or births, deaths, and marriages, next year can probably be predicted with greater accuracy than the average number of unemployed—even though we have discovered what " necessarily and inevitably determines the level of employment " but not the level of suicides.

Similarly, just as with regard to economic laws the argument is advanced, " But, of course, all laws in all sciences are hypothetical and take the form ' If p then q ' ", so with regard to prognoses it is argued that all prognoses rest on a ceteris paribus assumption : " Nobody in his senses would hold that the laws of mechanics were invalidated if an experiment designed to illustrate them were interrupted by an earthquake ",[41] it is insisted. But the prognoses of the other sciences are certainly not given in propositions of pure theory ; that is, they are *conceivably* falsifiable, and the ceteris paribus assumption—such as it *is* made—does not eliminate *all* falsifiability. To repeat that surely if the assumptions are given, then certain events *must* occur, is to repeat the analytical-tautological proposition, for these " events " are simply the " assumptions " or part of them under another name—just as the word " tariff " may be said to be another name for a particular kind of addition to a price.

The " *cetera* " in the natural sciences are either themselves also predictable according to known scientific laws, or else, like earthquakes in laboratories—which certainly appear not to be accurately predictable—have not in fact disturbed the overwhelming majority of laboratory experiments.

There is a further common distinction with regard to prognosis that seems apt to mislead ; that is the common distinction between " *qualitative* " and " *quantitative* " prognosis. The position represented seems to be that though " exact " and inevitable prognoses are reached by what is called the " qualitative " analysis of pure theory, it is futile and pretentious to attempt very much in the way of quantitative prognosis.[42] Though it can be said that under given conditions a price must inevitably rise, it cannot be said by *how much* it will rise. " Qualitative " prognosis here seems to mean simply a prognosis as to whether a rise or a fall in price will take place. But suppose a " qualitative " prognosis was made that a very small (if this is not a " quantitative " conception) rise in price would take place, and in fact (since it was a falsifiable prognosis that had been advanced, and not a proposition of pure theory) a very small *fall* in price occurred, this prognosis qualitatively would be false ; but considered quantitatively it might have been a brilliantly accurate prognosis, the resulting margin of error being relatively very small. Of course, what is meant by qualitative prognoses are the kind of " prognoses " given in propositions of pure theory which cannot conceivably be falsified. Why, however, cannot quantitative prognoses of this type also be made ? One only has to make the necessary quantitative assumptions and one can deduce the inevitable quantitative conclusions. But presumably the circular and question-begging character of the procedure would then become too plain. It is obviously true that only highly inexact (quantitative) prognoses can usually be made as regards economic events, but a false distinction does not seem the simplest way of bringing this out.

Leaving out of account, then, the kind of prognoses given by propositions of pure theory, it does not seem possible to give the terms " qualitative " and " quantitative " as applied to prognoses any more sense than " less accurate " or " more accurate ", and we suggest that their replacement by these terms would be less confusing. A corresponding false distinction seems to be involved when the attempt is sometimes made to differentiate between empirical and statistical investigations and conclusions. The former must always be in principle expressible in the more precise language of the latter.

There is finally the view to which the fullest and most penetrating discussion of Economic Prognosis led up : that all prognosis of economic events is impossible.[43] It was clearly seen that the prognostic content of propositions of pure theory was nil, but owing to the misconceived notions of exactness and necessity—" the all too human love of certainty ", as Pearson called it—all prognoses based on empirical regularities were objected to as in principle inexact and liable at any moment to be falsified. If all prognosis was really impossible, then those who hold that Economics is a non-empirical science just like Logic and Mathematics would at once be justified. Economics would be, as Pantaleoni put it, " an idle science but a true one ". For the applicability of pure theory to the facts of the world requires just those empirical regularities which are the basis for prognoses. As a matter of fact, all economic life, like all life, depends on a certain degree of successful predictability. It is difficult to imagine what a world would be like in which *no* predictions *at all* could be made. On the other hand, it is equally difficult to imagine what life would be like if the social sciences could make as perfect prognoses as the natural sciences. The impact of social science on

69

society, when and if there is a sufficiently considerable body of scientific doctrine to make any considerable impact, will be an infinitely more intricate subject of study than the impact of the natural sciences. Some kinds of sociological prognosis are obviously in themselves contradictory. If, for example, one was to make a full and accurate prognosis as to what kind of books were going to be written on Economics twenty, fifty, or one hundred years hence, one would have actually to write these books oneself, so that in the future they would only, so to speak, be reprints.[44]

But this is all too irrelevant to the present sociological position when the doctrines of economic science (as against economic pseudo-science) probably make little or no impact on society. At present economic scientists can, unfortunately perhaps, neglect the effects of their own doctrines, and can simply concentrate on gradually bit by bit increasing the accuracy or decreasing the inaccuracy of their necessarily highly uncertain prognoses, without undue concern about these much wider and more indefinite possibilities.

The possibility of prognosis in Economics is based on or intimately connected with the problem of causality in economic events. Here again we find attempts to give propositions of pure theory empirical content, and their being interpreted as stating causal relations—the causal analysis being similar to that given by Molière's doctor, who explained the soporific effects of a drug by its sleep-bringing power. A concept is *defined* so as to be related to another in a particular way, and then later on a change in the former is said to *cause* the—*ex definitione*—corresponding change in the latter.[45]

On the other hand other theories are, with doubtful relevance, criticised as *not* stating causal relations. In his well-known work Professor Mayer criticises the mathematically formulated " functional " price theories of Pareto, Cassel, and their predecessors as not stating *causal* relations but simply *functional* interdependencies.[46] But the formulation of causal relations in terms of functional interdependence is precisely the aim of the more advanced sciences which have got beyond the imprecise concepts of cause and effect.[47] It is not because they formulate the relationships between the quantities concerned in terms of functional interdependencies that these theories are unsatisfactory, but because the assumptions on which they are based are not in the least clear and are probably far more abstract and " unrealistic " than the propounders of the theories in question appeared to believe. Lacking, thus, any clear link with the facts of economic life which would break into their circularity, these theories hang in the air with no clear empirical content. But all this is criticism which can be levelled quite as fairly at the non-mathematical, non-" functional " theories of price and value, and not only at the non-Austrian theories selected by Professor Mayer.

We have been using the word " cause " up till now in that vague, imprecise way which usually gives no trouble in everyday conversation. But, for scientific purposes, a very precise definition must be given if the term is to be of use. This has been difficult enough to give even for the physical sciences, which in any case as they advance abandon the cruder conception of causal relations for that of functional interdependence. In the social sciences, though undoubtedly the concept, elusive as it is, is useful and even perhaps necessary, at any rate in the preliminary formulations of a scientific explanation, it seems almost impossible to render the concept at all precise.[48] It is all the more necessary, therefore, particularly when problems of causation are being disputed—as in controversies over the trade cycle they so often are—for the disputants to beware of simply beating the air either because they are using the term " cause " in different senses, or because one or other could not say at all precisely in what sense he is using it. A similar danger is obviously acute in the frequent controversies as to whether certain events are "*symptoms*" or "*causes*" of other events, or whether they are "superficial" causes or "real underlying" *causae causantes*. When event A is stated to cause or to have caused event B, or, as it is sometimes put, event A " plays or has played an important causal rôle, along with other factors, in bringing about B ", it is reasonable and advisable to enquire always with precisely what conceivably obtainable statistics these statements could be verified. Sometimes it is the causes of a particular event or series of events—for example, the world depression—that are argued over, sometimes it is some generalisation : " the causes of the trade cycle are pure monetary ".

It certainly is not at all clear precisely what the term " cause " signifies in such propositions as these or precisely how they are to be verified. We certainly do not volunteer here to give any other meaning to concepts like " the causes of a trade depression " than, simply, " certain events immediately preceding or accompanying a trade depression ".

## 4. THE " OPTIMISTIC " APPROACH AND THE PRESENT POSITION OF ECONOMICS

The method of approach of all the great systems of equilibrium theory—those of Clark, Marshall, Pareto, Wieser, and Wicksell—in fact the traditional method of the economic theorist, was variously known as that of " decreasing abstraction ", " successive approximations ", or the " isolating " one-at-a-time procedure. This approach was probably worked out most perfectly by Wieser. More recently it has been advocated under the name of the " optimistic " approach.[49]

According to this method deductions are first made from very " simple " postulates descriptive of model communities quite unlike our own. Then the postulates are gradually made less simple and more descriptive of the economic conditions of a contemporary community. The precise simplifying assumptions on which the different equilibrium systems were worked out were not always fully and quite unambiguously stated, but they appear to have included on the one hand some postulate as to money and expectation— whether it was some form of " neutral " money or that there was no money at all still seems not definitely settled [50]—and on the other hand they seem to have postulated conditions of perfect competition. In any case the aim of theoretical economists in recent years might, it appears, be fairly described as an attempt, in accordance with the " optimistic " procedure, somehow to extend the range and render more " realistic " the equilibrium systems in two main directions : *first*, by substituting for the deductions from the postulate of competitive market conditions deductions from postulates of " imperfect "

73

or monopolistic competition, and *secondly* to link the deductions of the equilibrium system with those of the theory of money and fluctuations by revising the postulate—whatever precisely it was—concerning money.[51]

In the next chapter the assumptions of equilibrium analysis are examined more fully. We simply wish to raise here one or two preliminary questions that have already occurred as to the serviceability of the " optimistic " procedure in this situation.

The two questions which at once occur to one are these : First, if one is going to revise the former assumptions—whatever they were—in favour of assumptions more nearly descriptive of the economic life of a contemporary community, how is one to find out, without the most extensive statistical investigation, precisely what these assumptions are—for example, as to the behaviour of trade unions and central bank directors—which are necessary for a theory of money and employment ? Presumably the answer is that this is a task for the empirical-statistical investigator (whether he is to be called an economist or not). But then the second question arises : Given that the statisticians have furnished one with answers, is there any reason at all for supposing that these assumptions will yield any significant chain of deductive conclusions ? The postulates of the equilibrium system were specially chosen for their " tractability "—as Mrs. Robinson calls the possibility of deducing chains of conclusions from them—rather than for their correspondence with the facts : that is the essence of the optimistic procedure. Why should the more realistic postulates continue to be tractable ? In any case, if the statisticians were to succeed in setting out a fairly compact series of broadly true "assumptions" descriptive of the economic life of the world, would not these themselves give us the laws of Economics, and would there then be very much left, and if so what, for the deductive " pure theorist " to perform ?

We may tentatively seek an answer to these questions by considering the immediate position of these attempts to extend the equilibrium systems. Leaving the consideration of the postulates of imperfect competition to the following chapter, we may consider very briefly the position of " dynamic " theories of money and employment.

One of the themes of almost every general treatment of the position of economic theory for decades now has been the necessity for replacing the " static " equilibrium analysis by some " dynamic " system. Thirty years ago Professor Schumpeter could write that only static theory has so far been to some extent satisfactorily worked out and that dynamics is a " land of the future ".[52] In fact, the very writers who completed the static equilibrium systems already insisted on the next step forward to " dynamics ". Just the same exhortations continue to be made to advance beyond the limited static analysis, but they cannot yet be said to have been answered very effectively. In fact, as to the recent attempts at dynamic pure theory it was generalised : " Formal modifications of equilibrium theory and particularly the variation suggested by the ' risk-theorists ' find the ideal of abstract description in the perfect logical circle, i.e. a closed deduction leaving no gaps where an analysis of change or causality can be introduced. The setting is thus a priori tautologous ; it arrives at results which are exactly identical with the elements of thought which have been put into the argument." [53]

What has prevented the " optimistic " procedure being set smoothly forward as explained, gradually advancing from the more simplified to the more " realistic " postulates ? What has gone wrong with the programme that Professor Mayer, for example, can recently speak of the difficulties of the transition from static to dynamic analysis as " almost insuperable " ? [54]

We cannot yet give any conclusive answer to these questions as to the serviceability of the " optimistic " procedure—the traditional procedure of theoretical economists—until we have examined more thoroughly the postulates of economic theory.

### NOTES

1. Cf. L. C. Robbins, *Nature and Significance of Economic Science*, 1st edition, p. 33 ; R. Strigl, *Die Ökonomischen Kategorien*, Kapitel 1 ; and the discussion in L. M. Fraser, *Economic Thought and Language*, p. 21 ff. It is presumably a similar definition that F. H. Knight has in view when he says (*Ethics of Competition*, p. 281) that " the laws of economics are independent of (a) wants, (b) resources, (c) technology ".

2. Cf. A. Amonn, *Zeitschrift für Nationalökonomie*, 1936, p. 313 : " Nein, unsere Wissenschaft ' studiert ' keineswegs menschliches Verhalten, sondern das menschliche Verhalten ist für sie ein Datum ".

3. Cf. M. Pantaleoni, *Pure Economics*, p. 4.

4. Cf. R. Strigl, *op. cit.* pp. 19-20.

5. Cf. L. von Mises, *Grundprobleme der Nationalökonomie*, *passim.* What it is desirable that Professor von Mises and his followers should show is how a proposition can possess empirical content and significance and not at the same time exclude any conceivable occurrence, that is, be unfalsifiable empirically.

6. See below, IV. 2.

7. Cf. J. Schumpeter, *Epochen der Dogmen- und Methoden-geschichte*, p. 46.

8. Cf. S. Bailey, *A Critical Dissertation on Value*, p. 254, and G. Myrdal, *Das politische Element in der nationalökonomischen Doktrinbildung*, pp. 110-11 : " Ein sorgfältiges Studium der positiven Ausführungen Ricardos über den Realwert und den unveränderten Wertmesser in seinen ' Principles ' zeigt ebenso, dass er ständig voraussetzt, was er beweisen will. . . . Ebenso läuft Ricardos breite Diskussion des Unterschiedes von ' values ' und ' riches ' auch nur auf fortgesetzte Tautologien hinaus."

9. Cf. P. Wicksteed, *Common Sense of Political Economy*, pp. 569 and 790.

10. Cf. R. F. Harrod, *Economic Journal*, 1934, p. 21 ; E. von Böhm-Bawerk, *Kapital und Kapitalzins*, 3, A, Band II. p. 645.

11. Cf. J. E. Cairnes, *Some Leading Principles of Political Economy*, p. 21. It is interesting to find precisely the same criticism in precisely the same form, *mutatis mutandis*, made by Professor Haberler of Mr. Keynes's theory of the " Multiplier " : *Zeitschrift für Nationalökonomie*, 1936, p. 300 ff.

12. Cf. B. M. Anderson, *Social Value*, pp. 41 and 45, and H. J. Davenport, *Value and Distribution*, p. 300 : " . . . the general understanding of the Austrian theory has come to be that it explains market value by marginal utility, and resolves marginal utility into market value ". Also p. 329.

13. Cf. E. Schams, *Jahrbuch für Nationalökonomie und Statistik*, 1927, p. 392, and M. H. Dobb, *Political Economy and Capitalism*, p. 151.

14. Cf. H. Mayer, " Der Erkenntniswert der funktionellen Preistheorien ", in *Wirtschaftstheorie der Gegenwart*, Bd. II.

15. Cf. A. Marshall, *Principles of Economics*, 8th edition, pp. 410 and 518. (See below, IV. 3.)

16. Cf. T. Veblen, *The Place of Science in Modern Civilization*, p. 203, and F. H. Knight, *Risk, Uncertainty and Profit*, p. 116 n.

17. Cf. J. Schumpeter, *op. cit.* p. 43. Halévy, *Growth of Philosophic Radicalism*, pp. 267-70, interestingly points out how the conception of economic law adopted by the classical economists was the victor in a struggle between French Physiocracy and Humean empiricism. In Adam Smith the struggle was unresolved. In Ricardo the former was finally victorious : " Now, the physiocrats did in fact borrow their notion of economic law from Christian theology, and, more exactly from Malebranche's theology from which there are barely disguised quotations in Quesnay, and which is expressly quoted by La Rivière ". The modern

conception of economic law is therefore a theological rather than a scientific one.

18. Cf. A. Amonn, *Ricardo als Begründer der theoretischen Nationalökonomie*, and J. B. Clark, *Distribution of Wealth*, pp. v-vi : " The term ' natural ' as used by classical economists in connection with standards of value, wages and interest, was unconsciously employed as an equivalent of the term ' static ' ".

19. Cf. C. Menger, *Untersuchungen über die Methode*, pp. 38-57, and *Die Irrtümer des Historismus*. On " exactness ", v. F. Kaufmann, *Methodenlehre der Sozialwissenschaften*, pp. 69 and 151.

20. Cf. G. Schmoller, *Jahrbuch*, 1883, p. 979.

21. Cf. L. Robbins, *op. cit.* pp. 118 and 110. As a mathematical economist puts it : " Les lois économiques sont par leur nature même des lois mathématiques " (H. L. Moret, *L'Emploi des mathématiques en économie politique*, p. 13). Cf. also H. D. Henderson, *Supply and Demand*, p. 17.

22. Cf. W. Sombart, *Die Drei Nationalökonomien*, p. 261. Economists have sometimes found themselves in the position of J. B. Say, who set out to explain the empirical phenomenon of " overproduction ", and discovered his " law " that it could not occur,—his " law " so far as it had any clear sense being simply an analytical proposition or definition which does not say anything about what happens or could conceivably happen to anything, excluding simply the inconceivable.

23. Cf. M. Pantaleoni, *op. cit.* p. 5.

24. Cf. L. von Mises, *op. cit.* p. 83.

25. Cf. W. S. Jevons, *Principles of Science*, vol. ii. p. 430 : " A law of nature as I regard the meaning of the expression, is not a uniformity which must be obeyed by all objects, but merely a uniformity which is as a matter of fact obeyed by those objects which have come beneath our observation. There is nothing whatever incompatible with logic and the discovery of objects which should prove exceptions to laws of nature " ; and V. Pareto, *The Mind of Society*, p. 35. Also recently M. H. Dobb, *op. cit.* pp. 178 and 279.

26. Cf. A. Marshall, *op. cit.* pp. 31-6.

27. Cf. E. Mach, *Erkenntnis und Irrtum*, 3, A, p. 450.

28. Cf. H. Bernadelli, *Die Grundlagen der ökonomischen Theorie*, p. 74, and J. Schumpeter, *Archiv für Sozialwissenschaft und Sozialpolitik*, 1916, p. 1 ff.

29. Cf. O. Morgenstern, *The Limits of Economics*, p. 66.

30. Cf. R. W. Souter, *Prolegomena to Relativity Economics*, p. 162 ; and on the other hand, F. Kaufmann, *op. cit*, p. 62 ff.

31. See above, II. 1.

32. Cf. L. M. Fraser, *op. cit.* pp. 52 ff.

33. See above, II. 1.

34. Cf. C. D. Broad, quoted by L. S. Stebbing, *A Modern Introduction to Logic*, 2nd edition, p. 408 : " Whilst the inductions of all advanced sciences make great use of deduction, they can never be reduced without residue to that process ".

35. Cf. N. R. Campbell, *What is Science?* p. 47.

36. Cf. C. G. Hempel and P. Oppenheim, *Der Typusbegriff im Lichte der neuen Logik*, p. 102.

37. Cf. F. H. Knight, *op. cit.* p. 14.

38. Cf. L. Robbins, *op. cit.* p. 111.

39. Cf. F. A. von Hayek, *Monetary Theory and the Trade Cycle*, p. 37.

40. Quoted by C. Leslie, *Essays*, p. 202. Leslie's comments are very apt.

41. Cf. L. Robbins, *op. cit.* p. 112. Cf. also F. Lutz, *Das Konjunkturproblem in der Nationalökonomie*, p. 134.

42. Cf. L. von Mises, *op. cit.* p. 113 : " Die Nationalökonomie als theoretische Wissenschaft kann keine andere als qualitative Erkenntnis vermitteln ; quantitative Erkenntnis kann immer nur die Wirtschaftsgeschichte ex post geben ".

43. Cf. O. Morgenstern, *Wirtschaftsprognose, passim*, and E. Schams, *Zeitschrift für Nationalökonomie*, 1934, p. 617.

44. Cf. O. Neurath, *Empirische Soziologie*, Kap. 10.

45. Cf. G. Haberler, *Zeitschrift für Nationalökonomie*, 1936, p. 301 : " The mistake of treating relationships by definition as causal relationships occurs rather frequently in economics ".

46. Cf. H. Mayer, *op. cit.*

47. Cf. B. Russell, *Mysticism and Logic*, p. 180 ff. ; M. Schlick, *Die Naturwissenschaften*, 1931, p. 145 ff. ; and P. Bridgeman, *The Logic of Modern Physics*, p. 60.

48. Cf. L. S. Stebbing, *op. cit.* p. 289.

49. Cf. J. Robinson, *Economics is a Serious Subject*, p. 6, and *Economics of Imperfect Competition*, p. 327 ; an " optimist " appears to be " an *analytical* economist who is prepared to work stage by stage towards the still far-distant ideal of constructing an *analysis* which will be capable of solving the problems presented by the real word ". (Our italics.)

50. Cf. J. R. Hicks, *Zeitschrift für Nationalökonomie*, 1933, p. 440 ff.

51. Cf. F. A. von Hayek, *Monetary Theory and the Trade Cycle*, chs. i. and ii.

52. Cf. J. Schumpeter, *Das Wesen und der Hauptinhalt der theoretischen Nationalökonomie*, p. 183.

53. Cf. J. Ackermann, *Econometrica*, 1936, p. 118.

54. Cf. H. Mayer, *op. cit.* p. 188, and F. H. Knight, *Zeitschrift für Nationalökonomie*, 1934, p. 7.

# IV

# THE BASIC POSTULATES OF PURE THEORY:
# EXPECTATIONS, RATIONAL CONDUCT,
# AND EQUILIBRIUM

1. " *Um so merkwürdiger ist es, dass sich in der gesamten Literatur weder genaue noch vollständige Angaben über die der Theorie vom allgemeinen Gleichgewicht zugrunde liegenden Annahmen in ordentlicher Weise zusammengestellt finden.*"

O. MORGENSTERN
Zeitschrift für Nationalökonomie, 1935

2. " *For if orthodox economics is at fault, the error is to be found not in the superstructure, which has been erected with great care for logical consistency, but in a lack of clearness and of generality in the premisses.*" J. M. KEYNES
(Preface) The General Theory
of Employment, Interest and Money

3. " *Es ist der Glaube an ein solches objektiv und ausserpreisbildungsmässig bestimmbares normatives ' Prinzip ' in der nationalökonomischen Theorie ganz tief eingewurzelt. Es kehrt dieses Prinzip unter allen möglichen und unmöglichen Bezeichnungen in unzähligen Argumenten wieder als ' Prinzip der Wirtschaftlichkeit ', ' Prinzip des kleinsten Mittels ', ' ökonomisches Prinzip ', ' rein*

81

*wirtschaftlicher Gesichtspunkt* ', *und in mannig-*
*fachen anderen Formulierungen. Natürlich gibt es*
*so etwas nicht.*"               G. MACKENROTH
Theoretische Grundlagen der
Preisbildungsforschung und Preispolitik


4. " *Il y a longtemps que personne ne songe plus à*
*devancer l'expérience, ou à construire le monde de*
*toutes pièces sur quelques hypothèses hâtives. De*
*toutes ces constructions où l'on se complaisait*
*encore naïvement il y a un siècle, il ne reste plus*
*aujourd'hui que des ruines.*"

HENRI POINCARÉ
La Valeur de la Science

# IV

## THE BASIC POSTULATES OF PURE THEORY
### EXPECTATIONS, RATIONAL CONDUCT,
### AND EQUILIBRIUM

### 1. THE " FUNDAMENTAL ASSUMPTION "

THROUGHOUT its history, the idea of some " Fundamental Assumption ", some basic " Economic Principle " about human conduct from which much or most of Economics can ultimately be deduced, has been deeply rooted in the procedure of economic theory. Some such notion is still, in many quarters, dominant at the present time. For example, it has recently been stated that the task of Economics is " to display the structure and working of the economic cosmos as an outgrowth of the maximum principle ".[1] This " fundamental maximum principle ", which should obviously receive very careful formulation and empirical verification, has been framed in different ways in the history of economic theory, from the profit-seeking Ricardian business man down to the " rational " consumer balancing marginal utilities. Sometimes more emphasis has been laid on the purely hypothetical nature of the principle as a starting-point for a deductive argument, while sometimes it is urged rather that the principle is in fact, roughly at any rate, an empirically true generalisation.[2]

But at the present day, far from there appearing to be any definite agreement as to the precise formulation of this " Fundamental Assumption ", there appears not even to be complete agreement as to whether it is necessary or in fact used at all.[3] The clarification of these problems, and the resolving of the at any rate superficial contradiction in the procedure of text-books which begin their exposition of the theory of value with the assumption that everyone acts " rationally " or " sensibly ", and then in a later chapter base their explanation of economic fluctuations on " mistakes ", fluctuations of optimism and pessimism, or the casino-like nature of the capital market, is a necessary preliminary to the task of co-ordinating the theory of output and employment with the theory of price or value. For this co-ordination, if it can usefully be carried through at all, can only take place by bringing the two theories under a common set of assumptions, which involves finding out and formulating more precisely what the assumptions of the two theories are.[4]

## 2. " PERFECT EXPECTATION " AND THE FUNDAMENTAL ASSUMPTION

In spite of other variations there is one remarkable characteristic common to nearly all formulations of the " Fundamental Principle " from its origins in Utilitarian doctrines down to the present time. One of Bentham's formulations was : " Nature has placed mankind under the governance of two sovereign masters, pain and pleasure. It is for them alone to point out what we ought to do, as well as to determine what we shall do ".[5] Ricardo expressed the principle in a particular connection thus : " Whilst every man is free to employ his capital where he pleases, he will naturally seek for it that employment which is most advantageous ; he will naturally be dissatisfied with a profit of 10 per cent, if by removing his capital he can obtain a profit of 15 per cent ".[6] J. S. Mill speaks of the fundamental assumption " that man is a being who is determined, by the necessity of his nature, to prefer a greater portion of wealth to a smaller in all cases. . . ." [7] Finally, a modern formulation : " The fundamental assumption of economic analysis is that every individual acts in a sensible manner, and it is sensible for the individual to balance marginal cost against marginal gain . . . sensible conduct leads to the maximisation of money gains ".[8]

The common characteristic of all these different formulations—chosen quite at random—of the Fundamental Assumption, is that as they stand they appear further to postulate, and only are applicable if the further postulate is made, that all expectations are perfectly correct. They therefore pass over all the problems of economy in the world as it is, which may be said to arise from precisely this factor of uncertainty and imperfect foresight. They all make no mention of the question *how* one is to maximise one's returns. They simply say that it is " rational ", " sensible ", or " natural " to do this, assuming, presumably, that one *knows* how this can be done. To decisions which are not of this certain automatic kind they have no applicability. The absence of uncertainty in the conditions analysed emerges clearly from the formulae themselves. According to Bentham, pleasure and pain completely determine one's actions. There is no question as to *which* line of conduct leads to pleasure and which to pain—this is apparently known for certain. Similarly with Ricardo, there is no uncertainty as to the relative advantages of different lines of investment. The assumption is tacitly made that it is perfectly foreseen that one will yield 10 per cent and the other 15 per cent, and people " naturally " select 15 per cent. With Mill again the problem as to *which* line of conduct will yield " the greater portion of wealth " is not mentioned as existing, and his principle that men " naturally " prefer this to a smaller portion only begins to have sense when it is assumed that people can foresee perfectly which line of conduct leads to the greater portion—an assumption which Mill apparently tacitly slips in. Again, in the last quotation there is, as it stands, no question as to *how* one is to maximise one's money gains. This is known, and one simply acts " sensibly " on one's certain knowledge.

Where uncertainty is present, as is in principle the case with any piece of conduct in this world, economic or otherwise, one cannot, strictly speaking, seek the most advantageous employment for one's capital or act so as to maximise one's returns. One can only act in accordance with one's *expectations* as to the " maximum " conduct, and the expectations of the most clever and " rational " may, in the world as it is, turn out to be incorrect. The terms " sensible " and " rational " cannot, then, be applied to conduct under conditions of perfect foresight in the same sense in which they are usually loosely applied to conduct in the world as it is. It is taken for granted as " natural " that people prefer a greater satisfaction, in the widest sense, to a lesser one when they *know for certain* which line of conduct leads to the greater and which to the lesser. But in the world as it is, where this is not known, the terms " rational " and " sensible " are usually applied to the *expectations or the process of arriving at the expectations* that one line of conduct will yield more satisfaction than an alternative. When an investment is called " stupid " or " irrational " it is not usually meant that the investor in question was deliberately aiming at less than the maximum return open to him, but that it was " stupid " of him *to expect* that he would maximise his returns in that way. This use of such terms is, of course, excluded from application under conditions where *all* expectations are alike perfect.

So long as one is concerned with a world where the choice is always an automatic one between a return which is *certainly* maximum and others which are *certainly* smaller, the assumption that people *expect* to maximise their returns and the assumption that they *actually do* maximise them come to the same thing. But where the consequences of all decisions can be perfectly foreseen, the maximum principle clearly works itself out in a very special way which must be fundamentally distinguished from the only way in which it can work itself out when there is any uncertainty present, that is, under conditions where people cannot conceivably *know* or *calculate* but can only more or less vaguely *guess*, which out of many possible lines of conduct will lead to the fulfilment of the principle. This vital distinction is only glossed over by assuming that people " tend " or " seek " to fulfil the maximum principle, and has been entirely passed over even when this principle has been formulated with the term "expect".[9] An analysis of a world with any uncertainty in it, and particularly an analysis which takes into account the factor of money (which can be construed as a sign that uncertainty is present, or even as a measure of its amount),[10] cannot start from the same assumption of "sensible" or "rational" conduct as that applicable in a world without uncertainty, with which, consciously and explicitly or not, the bulk of pure economic theory from Ricardo onwards appears to have been concerned.

With uncertainty absent, economic life is "problemless" and automatic, and people would become more or less automata. As Professor Knight has pointed out: "With uncertainty absent, man's energies are devoted altogether to doing things; it is doubtful whether intelligence itself would exist in such a situation; in a world so built, it seems likely that all organic readjustment would become mechanical, all organisms automata".[11] The Economic Man had perfect expectation. He was a pleasure machine because his life was purely mechanical.[12] To say that this sort of conceptual marionette manipulated by the theoretical economist as a preliminary thought-clearing exercise is "rational" or "has perfect foresight" is apt to be misleading. One might as well speak of the parts of a mechanical model "acting sensibly" or "having perfect expectation" when the mechanism works smoothly as designed.[13]

The problemless mechanical nature of the conditions analysed by the usual Theory of Value is brought out very clearly in the following description of its procedure: "When the fundamental assumption" (that everyone acts sensibly and maximises

88

his returns) " is made, every economic tendency can be analysed by a series of questions. What would a sensible man do in such a case ? . . . A technique which would study the economic effects of neuroses and confused thinking would be considerably more complicated than the technique here set out." [14] The Theory of Value, that is, is confined to economic tendencies where there is one definite, unambiguous, and correct answer to the question " How am I to maximise my returns ? "—conditions in which it might fairly be called neurotic or confused not to maximise them. It is inapplicable where there is any uncertainty about the answer to this question —which is, in principle, always the case in the world as it is.[15] Anyone in the world as it is, even the most brilliant economist, would be grateful for any information which would lead to his maximising his returns, and all he can do is to act in the way which he *expects* will maximise them, and can hardly be called neurotic or confused if his expectations are wrong. As Wicksteed put it : " We are bound to act upon estimates of the future, and since wise as well as foolish estimates may be falsified, the mere failure of correspondence between the forecast and the event does not in itself show that the forecast was an unwise one ".[16]

Passing over the difficulties in the interpretation of the term " wealth ", it may perhaps be a broadly true generalisation " that everyone desires to obtain additional wealth with as little sacrifice as possible ",[17] or " that every person will choose the greater apparent good ",[18] or that " man directs his actions so as to maximise the sum of his satisfaction ".[19] But this tells one nothing as to how, in fact, they set about fulfilling their desires, or, dropping the assumption of perfect expectation, how even it is "sensible" or "rational" for them to do so.[20]

### 3. THE DEMAND FOR CAPITAL GOODS AND FOR CONSUMPTION GOODS UNDER THE FUNDAMENTAL ASSUMPTION

There has recently been much discussion of expectation and uncertainty as affecting the demand for capital instruments. Here the attempt to make use of a definition of " rational " conduct which only has sense when perfect foresight is also assumed, has been found to lead to a more or less useless circular theory of interest. If it is *known for certain*—as Ricardo apparently tacitly assumed his entrepreneur knew for certain—that an extra £100 worth of machinery will add £3 annually to net output, and if the investors are acting " sensibly ", and applying the machinery everywhere just up to the point where it pays and only just pays, then the rate of interest is 3 per cent per annum.[21] The weak link in this circular chain (perfectly descriptive of a world with no uncertainty, but defined to include interest) is that obviously investors actually *never do nor can know* how much an additional £100 worth of machinery will yield, and can only act on their *expectations*: " The most important confusion concerning the meaning and significance of the marginal efficiency of capital has ensued on the failure to see that it depends on the *prospective* yield of capital and not merely on its current yield." [22] This is clearly traceable to the inappropriate use of a definition of " rational " conduct which tacitly assumes perfect foresight. But as is frequently pointed out in discussions of the definitions of " capital " and " consumption " goods, the defining line between the two must be very arbitrarily drawn —at any rate if one is drawing one's distinction in accordance with the length of the period of time which the good takes to consume. There is a " capital " element in *all* goods, in that all goods take *some* time to consume. The act of purchase and the act of consumption of a good cannot be coterminous in time. This can conveniently be made part of the definition of the term " consumption of a good or service ". Therefore expectations concerning the future must be considered as affecting the demand for " consumption " goods as well as that for " capital " goods. Risk, uncertainty, and more or less correct expectations about the future are not the peculiar characteristics of enterprise or capital investment, but pervade all action, economic or otherwise, in the world as we know it. The common text-book distinction between present goods and future goods (instead of more immediately and more distantly future goods) inaccurately neglects the complete continuity between the two. This not very obscure but fundamental point has been clearly put by Schönfeld : " Just as all economy is a provision for the future, so the determination of what is the economically most appropriate disposition of resources is something directed to the future. There is no difference in principle whether this future is immediate or remote. In this sense the disposition of resources for the so-called satisfaction of present needs is a provision for the immediate future." [23]

It is precisely because they take no account of the uncertainty factor that the analyses of " rational " consumers' behaviour, and " consumers' equilibrium ", where people balance the utility of one more lump of sugar against one more biscuit, seem so very fanciful and *wirklichkeitsfremd*. It is not necessarily because the quantities discussed are too small. If one is confronted with a chocolate, a cigarette, an aspirin tablet, and a biscuit (or even smaller quantities), of known quality, *to consume here and now*, one can arrange them fairly definitely in an order. But unless one can perfectly foresee one's tastes this time to-morrow or next week, in what order one will prefer such small quantities when the time comes to consume them can only be forecasted in the very roughest way.[24] The " perfect expectation " analysis of " rational " consumers' conduct is only very roughly applicable when, as is mostly the case, goods, first, take some time to consume, and secondly when the consumption is not begun as soon as the purchase is made—since in the intervening period anything may happen to upset one's calculations.[25]

So far we have been using an over-simplified notion of " the period of consumption " of a good. We have been considering only what may be called the period of " direct consumption " ; that is, the period of time at the end of which the good or service is physically worn out or used up. But " the period over which an object yields consumption is not necessarily that of its own existence as a good ".[26] It has been pointed out that the " period of production " of a glass of beer may be construed as in one sense going *back* to the Creation. So the " period of consumption " may be construed as extending *forward* to the Day of Judgment. Among the " net advantages " or disadvantages of a glass of beer may be that, by making one's driving unsteady, it may involve one in a fatal motor smash which will profoundly affect the lives of one's children, one's children's children, and so *ad infinitum*. There is no need to resort to far-fetched examples to demonstrate that any of one's most trivial everyday actions, economic or otherwise, may have indefinitely far-reaching consequential ramifications. So far as people take them into consideration at all, their economic decisions will be affected by more or less vague expectations as to the possibility of such ramifications.

The expectations, then, on which any economic decision is based *may* concern literally any conceivable event in the future history of the world. But corresponding to the distinction between " direct " and " indirect " periods of consumption, it may have some clarificatory value to distinguish between " direct " and " indirect " factors in expectation. By " *direct* " factors in expectation we mean expectation as to the bare physical and technical qualities of a good or service—of a box of cigars, a machine, or the work of a labourer. Such qualities are always *conceivably* capable of physical measurement at the end of the direct period of consumption when the good or service has been physically applied or used up. On the other hand " *indirect* " factors in expectation *may* relate to any conceivable occurrence either *during* the period of " direct " consumption, or at any time after it. Obvious " indirect " factors in expectation in relation to consumption goods are expectations as to the future of one's own tastes, and as to the future prices or obtainability of the goods if they are preservable (cf. food-hoarding against expected shortage). As regards capital instruments and labour, obvious " indirect " factors are the expected future prices of the goods they produce, and of the labour or capital instruments with which they are technically required to co-operate in production ; further, if there is any element of oligopoly, the further price policy of competitors may be considered. Finally it is clear that an individual's whole expenditure policy, and division of his income between " saving " and " consumption ", may well depend on what he expects his income to be in the future, which depends on his expectations as to the future of general economic conditions in his country, which depends on his expectations as to the future economic and political history of the world. (Compare the Victorian attitude to the future of the world and " saving " with that of to-day.)

## 4. "PERFECT EXPECTATION" AND EQUILIBRIUM

Though in most expositions of the Theory of Value any discussion of expectations has been completely lacking, several writers have argued that some such postulate as " perfect expectation " is necessary for equilibrium theory.[27] On the other hand, Professor Morgenstern [28] has shown that such a postulate may give a nonsensical indeterminate situation the very reverse of equilibrium. (Compare, for example, a game of chess in which both players foresaw each other's moves and tried to adjust their own accordingly, or else foresaw *their own moves as well* but by some fatal Cassandra-like compulsion were not able to alter them even if leading to defeat.) Professor Morgenstern goes on to argue that the theory of equilibrium must somehow get on without this postulate if it is not to collapse in a contradiction, and comments : " wie unüberlegt in der theoretischen

Ökonomie oft von grundlegenden Annahmen dort gesprochen wird, wo es lediglich um Unsinn handelt ". So far no attempt appears to have been made either to contest these conclusions or to show how equilibrium theory can dispense with the " perfect expectation " postulate.

It is important to notice that the " perfect expectation " postulate is not a postulate as to how people under conditions of equilibrium actually behave, but is introduced simply as an *explanation* of their behaviour. It is the general answer one would receive if one was able to question members of a community in static equilibrium as to how they came to behave in the way they did. What is necessary for equilibrium is only that people behave in a certain way, and it is not strictly necessary to go into the question as to how or why they should behave in this way any more than with any other hypothetical simplified example. The case has been considered of a community producing· and consuming only one commodity [29]—bananas—and it is not necessary to enter into the question as to how and why a community should live on such a diet. There may be no satisfactory answer as to how or why they should behave in this way ; it is enough for the purposes of the simplified example that they do. If we find that people could not possibly behave as in the simplified example—that is, live solely on bananas—and be constituted like ourselves, the contradiction does not lie in the example as such, but in our procedure. We create certain conceptual automata " motivated " necessarily in a way different from ourselves, and then, with unconscious anthropomorphism, try to ask them why it is they behave like that, while the only answer to such a question ultimately is that they do so because we make them when we define the position of equilibrium. It is as though one was to sketch out the plans for, or actually construct (as one could actually construct a mechanical model of a community in static equilibrium) some piece of mechanism, say a cuckoo clock, and then ask the cuckoo whether it was because it had perfect expectation of the time that it appeared exactly at each hour.[30]

In some cases the economist will consider it enough simply to ascertain what people's conduct in certain situations is, or to establish a correlation between it and other social phenomena. But in other cases, for a satisfactory scientific explanation the economist will want to ascertain how this conduct came about, that is, with what other conduct—" expectations " or " beliefs "—it was correlated, and how in turn these latter came to be held.[31] As, therefore, the equilibrium concept is designed to help in the explanation of people's behaviour as it is, and as *Gedankenexperimente* with extreme cases are sometimes useful for the analysis of the facts as they are, the anthropomorphising of the mechanical model by enquiry as to what "expectations" or "motives" the behaviour of an equilibrium community could reasonably be correlated with, may possess some clarificatory value provided we keep in mind its ultimate contradictoriness and the fact that people *might* behave in any particular way for any reasons, or without any particular reasons at all. For, at any rate at present, little is known of significance about the " reasons " behind different types of economic conduct. In any case, if one does not attribute expectations to a person one can hardly call his conduct " sensible " or " rational ".

Expectations are correlated with behaviour in the market in accordance with the maximum principle. A person forms particular expectations as to the future course of events (his tastes, prices, consumers' demand, etc.), and from these arrives at the expectation that a particular line of conduct will lead to the maximum returns. A person with perfect expectation is able at once to dispose of his resources in accordance with the principle that people act in the way which they expect will lead to the maximum returns, for his expectations will tell him certainly and unambiguously which line of conduct will lead to this result. This would not be possible where two or more people have perfect expectations about one another's conduct and then try to adjust their own conduct in accordance with the maximum principle. A game of chess or bridge with all players having perfect expectations of one another's play and then adjusting their own, could not be played.

The example might be put forward of two duopolists both of whom foresaw that the other possessed full knowledge of the theory of duopoly and was going to fix his price at the monopoly price, fixed their own prices at the monopoly price, and thus, in a certain sense, maximised their profits.[32] But this is not really a case of perfect expectation and consequent adjustment of conduct in accordance with the maximum principle. If one of the two duopolists perfectly foresees that his rival is going to fix his price at the monopoly price over a definite period of time—if this is *given* to him—he is not acting in accordance with the maximum principle in fixing his own price at the same level. If it is replied that he does not do this because he knows perfectly well that if he does not fix his own price at the monopoly price his rival will of course alter his correspondingly, then he had not originally perfect foresight as to his rival's price policy, for with perfect foresight he must have certainly known *un-conditionally* his rival's price policy over the period of time in question.

The impossibility of "monopolistic" conduct based on perfect expectations is not simply a high improbability but a *logical* impossibility, a self-contradictory paradox, like the Cretan saying that all Cretans are liars. A person's conduct cannot both be given to someone else who may adjust his own accordingly, and still be adjustable by the person himself. Just the same is the case if it is not a question of two individuals facing each other, but of each individual member of a mass facing the average opinion of the mass, as in Mr. Keynes'[33] description of the professional speculator working out what average opinion expects average opinion expects, average opinion expects . . . (etc. *ad infinitum*) future prices will be. The game of Old Maid —as Mr. Keynes describes speculation—obviously could not be played when each player had perfect expectation. For if they were seeking to maximise their profits and had control over their conduct, each player in turn whose perfect expectations told him he would have the Old Maid would not play.

Perfect expectation therefore is incompatible, in an interdependent economic system, with people acting in the way they expect will maximise their profits and at the same time more than one person adjusting his conduct in accordance with his (perfect) expectations of the other's conduct—that is, it is incompatible with more than one person acting "monopolistically" with perfect expectation.[34] Perfect expectation is only compatible with " competitive " conditions—that is, conditions where no one person's conduct can affect the conduct, and the result of the calculations on which it is based, of another.[35]

If, then, the assumption of perfect expectations, which appears to be implicit in many formulations of the " Fundamental Principle ", must be dropped for oligopolistic analysis, some other definite assumption about some sort of imperfect expectations and the correlated conduct must take its place, if any attempt at " explaining " oligopolists' conduct is to be made. If one's interests are purely geometrical or algebraical one need not worry about how one's demand and supply curves can be drawn up. But then it is hardly justifiable to call the conduct recorded by them " sensible " or to suppose that it *necessarily* ever occurs in practice; it is simply one out of an infinite number of types of conceivable behaviour. A " biologist " might pursue his science, not by enquiring what the laws of heredity or genetics are, but by working out an infinite number of conceivable formulae.

One might assume that though people are acting under oligopolistic conditions, where each individual's conduct has some appreciable effect on price and market conditions, they none of them take the effects of their own conduct on their rivals' conduct in any way into account.[36] That is, they behave like bridge-players who play the card which seems to them best without any consideration of the effects that their play has on the subsequent play of the other people at the table. Though such conduct may conceivably be " sensible " in the special sense of being based on the expectation that it will lead to the fulfilment of the maximum principle, such an expectation can hardly be called sensible in any less special sense of the term, nor does the assumption of it appear very realistic.

The difficulty is simply that under oligopolistic conditions there is no one clear and unambiguous answer to the question " How would a sensible man act in such a situation ? " [37] Such a question is not very helpful. His action all depends on his necessarily imperfect expectations about the conduct of other people. Though one can argue in a vague impressionist way *a priori* that some assumptions are more reasonable than others, if one wants to find out how or on what expectations oligopolists in fact behave, the only way is to " look and see ".[38] It cannot be directly deduced from some " Fundamental Principle ", any more than, except in a very few cases, one can deduce how a hand of bridge will be played, or even how it would be " rational " to play it, with given cards simply from the principle that all the players are " sensible " and are out to maximise their points. Outside competitive conditions, any " equilibrium " position or position of rest which may occur is a conventional one, arrived at along its own particular path—which might well have been different— and which will last just as long as the conventions which support it happen to last.

So far we have not attempted, in discussing perfect expectation, to decide whether or not it is the only condition of expectation which is reasonably correlatable with the behaviour of an individual or community in the condition of " equilibrium ". On the one hand there are various possible conditions which an individual or a community might be in, which might be called " equilibrium ". On the other hand it is necessary to distinguish clearly between *perfect*

expectation and simply *correct and undisappointed*
expectations.

" Perfect ", " correct ", and " undisappointed "
expectations appear often to have been used more
or less interchangeably as a necessary or even defining characteristic of equilibrium.[39] But in quite
ordinary senses of the words, " undisappointed "
expectations may well not have been " correct ",
and " correct " expectations may well not have been
" perfect ". By perfect expectation we mean, practically, omniscience about the future. A man with
perfect expectation must at least have certain knowledge about everything that is relevant to his decisions—and this *may* possibly be anything in the
whole future history of the world—and he must at
any rate know about everything else that it is irrelevant. On the other hand a man's expectations
as to the results of a line of conduct may be quite
*correct*, and he may also expect that he will maximise
his returns by adopting it, but he may not have heard
of other possibilities which would be more profitable
to him, and therefore, though his expectations about
the line of conduct he adopts are quite correct, he is
not acting in the most lucrative possible way. This
kind of blissful ignorance is probably a common condition. The distinction between " correct " and " undisappointed " expectations is of small importance. A
man's expectations about the line of conduct he
adopts may be quite correct and he may get exactly
what he counted on, but because *in the meantime*
possibilities have been suggested to him of which he
was ignorant before, he may be *disappointed* that he
did not act in another way.

But whether expectations are perfect or imperfect,

correct or incorrect, undisappointed or disappointed, has nothing whatever to do, logically, with whether they are *constant* or *changing*, and on this depends whether or not there is any change in an individual's conduct or any endogenous [40] change in an economic system. Expectations are constant when people believe that the expectations and the correlated conduct of the previous period will lead to the maximum returns in the next period. Whether expectations have just been incorrect or disappointed or the reverse does not imply either that they will be changed or held to, or, necessarily, that it would be " rational " to change or hold to them. Because of the tacit or explicit assumption of perfect expectation, endogenous changes, in the usual exposition of equilibrium analysis, appear generally to be regarded as more or less automatic. When the assumption of perfect expectation is dropped it is seen that whether or not there is an endogenous change depends on the much less automatic factor of whether people's expectations are constant or not. It is the assumption of perfect expectation, further, which brings it about that in the absence of other changes elsewhere there will be no further change in the disposition of resources when the position of equilibrium has been attained. When this assumption is removed this peculiar characteristic of the " equilibrium " position is also removed, for an (incorrect) change may be made in the disposition of resources which *would have been* in their " maximum " " equilibrium " position if it had not been made.

If expectations are perfect they must necessarily also be correct, undisappointed, in " static " conditions constant, and in " dynamic " conditions changing. Further, people with perfect expectation must be in their " maximum " position, that is, they could not obtain greater returns anywhere else. But if expectations are *not* perfect, any combination of one of the alternatives from each of the pairs, correct or incorrect, undisappointed or disappointed, constant or changing, is possible. If we drop the division of " correct " expectations into disappointed and undisappointed as being of little interest, this leaves eight possible conditions of expectations and correlated conduct—four when people are actually in their " maximum " positions, and four when they are not : correct and constant, correct and changing, incorrect and constant, incorrect and changing. For if expectations are not perfect it is quite possible for someone to be in his " maximum " position, not to realise it, be disappointed, and change. While in the world as it is nobody could be found with quite perfect expectations in our sense, a good number, probably, could be found in each of the eight " imperfect " conditions we have classified.

Any favourable or maximum position may be arrived at by " luck " or by " judgment " or by any mixture of the two. Though it might well happen that an *individual* was in his " maximum " position more or less by accident, that is, not having been led to it by perfect expectation, it is obviously fantastically improbable that all the members of a *community* could for any length of time be all in their respective maximum conditions by accident, *without* perfect expectation or a combination of luck and nearly perfect expectation. We agree therefore that, on the whole, perfect expectation is the most reasonable state of knowledge and expectation to be attributed

103

to, or correlated with, that harmonious optimum condition which has always been the ideal of Economic Liberalism. We agree, further, that the term " equilibrium " is best reserved for this condition, but we do not agree with making " perfect expectation " a *defining characteristic* of it.[41] For this involves defining " equilibrium ", not by the actions and conditions of an individual or community, but by the knowledge which led them to these actions and conditions. It seems that " equilibrium " is best reserved for the optimum maximum condition whether or not the individual or community has been led to it by perfect expectation.

There is one further slight ambiguity about the term " equilibrium ". In a sense, no single economic action takes place except when or where there is " disequilibrium ". " Equilibrium ", that is, only holds where there is, and so long as there is, complete inactivity. But the term seems often to be used of a condition lasting while economic action is taking place. That is, a community or individual is not necessarily in " disequilibrium " in the moment before any economic activity, if this activity is leading to the maximum returns.

## 5. THE ASSUMPTION OF A " TENDENCY " TOWARDS EQUILIBRIUM

The position of equilibrium has always been the very central concept of economic analysis. *A priori* one cannot say more than that this is just one out of an infinite number of conceivable positions. The only justification for the special concern with this position and the treatment of disequilibrium, change and development, as simply temporary aberrations from the normal, can be that in fact the economic conditions under which we live in some sense " tend " towards it. This is the very crux of equilibrium theory. Professor von Hayek goes as far as to say : " There seems to be no possible doubt that the only justification for this " (special concern with equilibrium analysis) " is the existence of a tendency towards equilibrium. It is only with this assertion that economics ceases to be an exercise in pure logic and becomes an empirical science."[42] Is this as a justification satisfactory ?

We have seen that the only way to make sense of most formulations of the Fundamental Assumption is to add the assumption of " perfect expectation ". With this assumption added we are assuming also, at the same time, permanent equilibrium under competitive conditions, and the disappearance of money. The early writers regarded the equilibrium condition —that is, complete expectations—as constantly at hand, as a position on which society was constantly verging.[43] Until fairly recently it was considered that if a comparison was made between economic life and the water in a tank which is constantly being disturbed, but which could soon sink to a position of " rest " when the disturbance was removed, enough had been said to justify almost exclusive preoccupation with equilibrium analysis.[44] It was overlooked that it is an experimentally testable empirical truth that water sinks to an equilibrium level if left undisturbed, while there is no corresponding empirical truth or even suggested experiment with regard to an economic system. To justify special preoccupation with the position of equilibrium it is necessary to assert as an empirically testable truth that there is a tendency towards this position in our economic system, or that readjustment in general comes quicker than new disturbances occur.

But there is an ambiguity in speaking of a " tendency towards " a certain condition which is not always kept clear in this connection. It may mean that the position *actually is* regularly arrived at, or it may simply mean that although there is a " tendency " towards this position, this " tendency " is always counterbalanced by other " tendencies " which result in the position never in fact being reached at all, or even necessarily approximated to. This is the sense in which to-day most economists appear to speak of the tendency towards equilibrium. For example : " We make no assumption that final equilibrium is necessary. We assume that there are operative in different parts of the system certain tendencies which make for the restoration of an equilibrium in respect to certain limited points of reference. But we do not assume that the composite effect of these tendencies will necessarily be equilibrating." [45]

This interpretation of the assumption of a " tendency towards equilibrium " at once gives away the case for any special preoccupation with this condition rather than with any other conceivable condition of the economic system. There is no assumption, here, that we necessarily ever come anywhere near an equilibrium condition. One might assume that there was a " tendency ", in this sense, for the population of England to dwindle to nothing (through diseases, wars, etc.), or to become indefinitely large (through births and a falling death-rate, etc.), or to attain to any other conceivable figures—though the

" tendencies " to these positions were always offset by opposing tendencies. If, therefore, the special study of the equilibrium position rather than any other conceivable position is to be justified by the empirical truth of the assumption of a "tendency" towards equilibrium, this must mean a tendency in the former, *significant* sense ; that is, it must be the case that we are always in equilibrium or fairly often approximating to it to make a special study of it of particular interest.[46] At least one is entitled to expect those who justify their special study of the equilibrium condition on the grounds— in their usual rather metaphysical language—that they are " examining in isolation a part of the forces acting in the real world ", to give some empirical indication as to the " strength " of these forces under existing conditions as compared with the strength of the opposing " forces ", or at least to make it clear that whether their analysis is of any conceivable application depends on this issue. It is hardly a sufficient justification of equilibrium analysis, and completely begs the question of its applicability, to claim—as someone engaged in the exclusive study of conditions in England with a population of 0, 1000, or 1,000,000,000 might claim—that, though it is of course counteracted by opposing " tendencies " so that the condition never sets in or is necessarily approximated to, there is always a " tendency " towards it.

The assumption of a tendency towards equilibrium implies, on the usual definition, the assumption of a tendency towards perfect expectations, competitive conditions, and the disappearance of money. To get anything like a precise answer to the question as to what extent this assumption is true or untrue would require vastly complicated empirical investigations. Possibly it was nearer the truth in the nineteenth century than it is to-day. In some markets, obviously expectations are more nearly perfect than in others. Probably the more "oligopolistic" markets become, the less perfect expectations become, for then there is an important addition to the number of factors about which, up till now at any rate, only fairly uncertain expectations can be formed—that is, the behaviour of rival oligopolists. The lengthening of the processes of production would also probably increase uncertainty and disequilibrium. On the other hand there is, on the whole, probably a tendency for communities to *learn*, which does more than simply keep pace with the changes in conditions. But whether ultimately, if more correct prognoses come to be made, these will not defeat their own end by themselves bringing about further changes and thus rendering themselves false, whether or how far, that is, there is a definite relation between the prognoses of social science and the social facts, remains an open sociological question which can hardly be of more than speculative interest until there are more data in the form of recognised and disseminated economic and sociological prognoses.

At present, at any rate, the "perfect expectation" assumption of equilibrium analysis begs all our questions, and we conclude with a recent investigator : "To attempt to retain the partial equilibrium approach by introducing such assumptions as ' the future is completely foreseen ' or that money remains neutral, amounts in effect to an exclusion of the whole problem. The question is on the contrary just to what degree, under realistic assumptions concern-

ing the anticipations of the entrepreneurs, the future
is shown to be foreseen, and furthermore, to what
extent total ' monetary ' categories disrupt the adjustment towards a partial equilibrium." [47]

## 6. " SUBJECTIVE " AND " OBJECTIVE " RATIONALITY

The "Fundamental Assumption" as usually formulated, if it is to have any sense, must be supplemented
by the assumption of perfect expectation. The
element in the " Fundamental Assumption " thus
formulated, in the Economic Man, in the " maximum
principle ", and the like, applicable to a world with
any uncertainty and imperfect foresight, that is, to
a world in which any *economic* as against perhaps
simply *technical* problems may be said to exist, is the
principle that people act in the way they *expect* will
maximise their returns, profits, or net advantages.
This is the " general " principle of which the assumption of perfect expectation is a very peculiar special
case. Everybody's conduct is in this sense " sub-
jectively " rational (though we use this term only at
once to suggest that it is misleading and unsuitable),
however " irrational " and nonsensical the *expectations* on which it is based. How far people act in
an " objectively " rational way must remain quite
indefinite, because in the first place, in a world full
of uncertainty and with economic science still able to
afford very little guidance, most decisions in economic
life *have* to be taken without recourse to anything
which can suitably be called " objective rationality "
—though it is in accordance with some such objective
criterion or other that the term is applied to expectations or the process of arriving at them in everyday life.

The term " rational " simply means, normally, being guided in a certain way by past experience ; the question is in precisely *what* way. A complete " objective rationality " in economic conduct requires a complete economic science which can tell one with " certainty " exactly what the effects of one decision or the other will be, and even then a sceptic can argue that it is not necessarily " rational " to act even in accordance with the most confirmed and certain of scientific prognoses. Nor can the calculus of probability, rather vaguely appealed to by Bentham and subsequent writers, be of the slightest assistance in most economic decisions, for there is simply no basis for any sort of calculation.[48] Judgments as to the " objective rationality " or " irrationality " of economic conduct or expectation can on the whole only be fragmentary and negative.

There is, however, one class of expectations, possibly not uncommon, which could quite definitely and objectively be called irrational—that is, *contradictory* expectations. Under uncertain conditions economic calculation—if it can be called that under such conditions, since the very term seems to imply some automatic " certain " basis—takes the form of considering the various relevant factors, direct and indirect, which occur to one in deciding one's choice, and then selecting that line of conduct which, given these expectations, will lead to the maximising of returns. If the expectations as to the various relevant factors—even simply those that happen to occur to one—are not sufficiently pondered, it is quite possible that all the *strictly logical implications* contained in them are not realised and are not seen to be in contradiction to the maximising

110

of returns by the line of conduct chosen. One of the expectations *must* be falsified then, and it will be pure luck if it is not that as to the maximising of returns.

The Law of Motivation,[49] as the principle of "subjective rationality " may more suitably be called, is undoubtedly the core of empirical truth in the Economic Man and similar generalisations about human conduct. Though we agree that there is no principle of any considerable significance that will serve as a basis for a realistic deductive economic theory, we do not, therefore, precisely agree with Professor Mackenroth that there is no such principle at all. It appears an empirically true and testable generalisation that people act in the way which they expect will maximise their returns, even if this was only the *ex post* rationalisation of their habits. This generalisation could, if it was worth while, be more precisely formulated and a more precise method of testing it be given. Roughly, one can test it simply by asking anyone whether they expect that if they were to employ their money or resources in any other way than that in which they are at the moment doing or about to do, they expect that they would increase their returns. If they reply that they *do* expect that they would increase their returns—understood, if one likes, in the widest sense to include the " satisfaction" of the masochist and altruist—by employing their resources in another way, then they are offending against the principle of subjective rationality or the Law of Motivation. But it would appear a waste of time for an economist, at any rate, to attempt to define this principle more precisely, as the significant content of this generalisation as a fundamental

111

assumption for a deductive economic theory is in any case negligible.

One can, of course, draw the usual conclusions that people will balance expected marginal cost against expected marginal gain, and will have no tendency to change their conduct when the expected marginal return from resources in each direction is equal, and so on. But out of an almost circular postulate only almost circular conclusions can be drawn. But what is always wanted is *what* expectations people have, that is, in what way they expect they will maximise their returns, and therefore in what way they will behave. This Law of Motivation tells one nothing whatever about this.

The orthodox " perfect expectation " Theory of Value was all more or less empty when it was based on the assumption that everyone maximised *his utility*, because of the difficulty in defining this term in any but a more or less circular and empty way. On the other hand, the principle seemed to have some content and to permit of deductions of some content about the behaviour of entrepreneurs, and their price, production, wage, and employment policies. For without too great inaccuracy entrepreneurs might be said to aim at maximising their money profits, which seemed a definite enough criterion to decide their policies (though even here, in the interests of accuracy, some economists are in favour of making this proposition more or less circular, insisting that the entrepreneurs' aim is not maximum money profits, but maximum satisfaction from the " net advantages "). Looked at retrospectively *ex post*, profits are a fairly definitely calculable sum. As, however, it is clearly not the " objective " resulting *ex post* profits but the " subjective " *ex ante* expectations which determine entrepreneurs' policy,[50] and which are in a common metaphor the " mainspring " of economic activity, unless one makes a definite assumption about expectations, " maximising profits " is quite an empty conception telling one nothing about how entrepreneurs will in fact behave. With the assumption of complete expectations no relevant distinction between *ex post* and *ex ante* profits existed, next year's profits being as definitely and objectively known as last year's. But dropping the assumption of complete expectations, the problem remains as to what expectations people hold and how they come to hold them. To make assumptions as to expectations and therefore as to conduct, unless these assumptions are empirically confirmed, is, in dealing with economic problems fundamentally, to beg the question and assume what one wants to find out, which is always just what people's expectations and correlated behaviour in different situations are.

It has long been recognised that, when economists assume that people behave " rationally ", no assumption is made as to the nature of the goods—bread, opium, bibles, or instruments of self-torture—which it is " rational " to choose, no such distinction being feasible. Similarly (as we have argued) no generalisation is possible either as to what is, in some sense, the *objectively rational* way of arriving at one's expectations, or as to *how people do, in fact,* arrive at their expectations that one line of expenditure will yield them better returns than another. Whether and to what extent entrepreneurs behave " competitively " or " monopolistically ",[51] whether and to what extent people's decisions are dominated by present prices as against the whole expected future course of prices ; to what extent people's economic actions are taken on the spur of the moment, or according to a detailed plan ; how far people come to any particular expectation at all or act unreflectingly according to habit ; to what extent people learn from past economic mistakes and disappointments ; how and to what extent people behave in any way one chooses to call objectively rational—are questions which cannot be answered by any general " Fundamental Assumption " or " Principle ". Although in some cases rough *a priori* reasoning may yield results which turn out fairly accurately when tested, *ultimately* all such questions as these can only be decided satisfactorily by extensive empirical investigation of each question individually.

The Law of Motivation says nothing about how people behave in any market, nor anything about the expectations or the process of arriving at the expectations correlated with behaviour in the market. It only says something as to how people will react if questioned in a particular way as to their behaviour in the market. It is, however, an empirical generalisation capable of being tested empirically and of being falsified, possessing therefore *some* empirical content, however insignificant this may be. It is not simply an empirically empty definition, which is what is sometimes offered as a " Fundamental Principle " of economic conduct.

## 7. THE FUNDAMENTAL ASSUMPTION AS A DEFINITION

Since the revolution in the Theory of Value of 1871 economists have been trying to formulate a fundamental " maximum principle " of economic conduct applicable to consumers, to take the place of the Ricardian business man guided only by the desire for money profits. To render this principle not obviously false they have had steadily to widen it, and thus to diminish its empirical content. First it had to be agreed that it was not necessarily " rational " for the consumer to seek to maximise merely his *material* wealth—" spiritual " wealth must also be included. Then in order to elude the charge of hedonism the conduct of altruists and masochists had to be admitted as " rational ". The economic principle thus became less and less falsifiable. Fewer and fewer, if any, types of economic conduct remained which were not subsumed under it, and almost none were excluded or could falsify it. Its empirical content, therefore, simultaneously grew smaller and smaller.[52] To say that a piece of economic conduct was " rational " came to mean little, if anything, more than that it was a piece of economic conduct. The cruder classical generalisations about the ubiquity of the money-making motive, though in a probably high percentage of cases false, did have some empirical significance. Ricardo's instinct was right when he wrote : [53] " It is self-interest which regulates all the speculations of trade ; and, where that can be clearly and satisfactorily ascertained, we should not know where to stop if we admitted any other rule of action ". He was wrong in believing apparently that self-interest could often with much accuracy be " clearly and satisfactorily ascertained ".

Finally it came to be openly stated that the " Fundamental Principle " was not conceivably falsifiable and devoid of *all* empirical content, a circularity, a matter of definition, a linguistic proposal. It was assumed or stated that everybody behaves " rationally " or " sensibly ", and " rationally " or " sensibly " was defined as how people do in fact behave. All economic conduct is *ex definitione* rational or sensible. It would be contradictory to speak of " irrational " economic conduct, or if one does " one means only that one's fellow men do not act as one considers right ".[54]

It is sometimes argued, even when it is thus stated as a circularity or definition, that the Fundamental Assumption cannot be empty because of all that economists have succeeded in deducing out of it.[55] Certainly its being a circularity does not preclude any number of deductions being made from it. But all the propositions thus deduced will be equally circular and empirically empty. If the Fundamental Assumption that everybody acts rationally is circular, so is the proposition that people balance marginal cost against marginal gain circular, and all the further deductions will simply be different ways of saying that people behave " rationally ", that is, as they do behave. If one thinks it worth while, one can say " people behave as they do behave " in as many different ways as one likes, but one will not learn anything further about their behaviour; for the empirical content of the assumption and all the conclusions will be the same—that is, nothing. " From a tautology only tautologies follow." [56]

With a definition there is no question of verifiability or falsifiability. One can, if one likes, say " Economic conduct = ' Rational ' or ' sensible ' economic conduct. Def.", if one is consistent in this linguistic usage. As a terminological suggestion, however, it simply seems superfluous, inappropriate, and misleading. It is superfluous, because if one takes economic behaviour as given, one's task is to examine it as it is, and there is no point in adding the adjective " rational " or " sensible ", which is *by definition* purely redundant. It is inappropriate because we all know—and this is often particularly emphasised precisely by those who insist that all economic conduct is or " must be " rational—that, in the everyday " objective " sense of the terms, much economic conduct is the very reverse of " rational " or " sensible " : that is, is based on quite incorrect and " stupid " expectations. Lastly it is misleading because it may appear that some generalisation of empirical content is being made about economic conduct from which conclusions of empirical content may be deduced, while all that is being done is to set out a definition.

In defence of this terminology it has been suggested that it is necessary to make it clear in this way that the Fundamental Principle of Economics is in no sense a value-utterance exalting any one type of economic conduct above another.[57] But it is not clear, to say the least, why, in order to exclude value-utterances concerning one piece of economic behaviour as compared with another, it is necessary to deliver what, in appearance at any rate, is a sweeping and vague value-utterance about *all* economic behaviour. It is like suggesting that a book-reviewer not wishing to deliver himself of value-utterances, cannot content himself with simply giving an account of books and the facts about them, but must insist that *all* books are, and " must be ", by definition good, or " rational " and " sensible " books.

## 8. A METHODOLOGICAL CONCLUSION

A broader methodological conclusion would appear to follow from the above. In so far as one is dissatisfied with purely " static ", a-monetary analysis omitting the uncertainty factor—which alone may be said to create any problems of conduct economic or otherwise—the method of deduction from some " Fundamental Assumption " or " principle " of economic conduct is more or less useless, because no relevant " Fundamental Assumption " can, on our present knowledge, be made.

The whole conception of Economics, as held for example by Senior, as a science resting on a very few general propositions (or " four Fundamental propositions ", the first being " that every person is desirous to obtain with as little sacrifice as possible, as much as possible of the articles of wealth "),[58] is shown to be entirely inadequate. Because the uncertainty factor was passed over it was possible to believe with Robert Lowe [59] that " If you place a man's ear within the ring of pounds, shillings and pence his conduct can be counted on to the greatest nicety ". Only so long as more or less tacit assumptions as to expectations were being made did the use of such a method as the deduction of chains of conclusions from one or a compact number of fundamental assumptions seem applicable. When assumptions as to expectations are more or less explicitly introduced, there come, quite rightly, accusations of " circularity ", " begging the question ", and " assuming what one requires to prove ", which have been a rather conspicuous feature of recent controversies over the theory of money and employment and the development of some kind of " dynamic " pure theory.[60]

According to Professor von Hayek,[61] the immediately pressing questions in this field are how entrepreneurs react to the expectations of particular price-changes, how the expectations of entrepreneurs are formed, and how given price-changes affect entrepreneurs' expectations. Clearly the answers to such questions cannot be deduced from some " Fundamental Assumption " or conjectured at all accurately *a priori*. They are questions of economic psychology to which an answer will be sought in vain in a few empty utilitarian phrases. If one wants to find out the answer to such questions, one must admit with Richard Jones : [62] " I really know of but one way to attain our object, and that is to look and see ". As a prominent investigator has recently concluded : " Thus, logically speaking, the door is open for all kinds of reactions ; and it is only a question of fact which one is the most frequent and typical ",[63] or as another puts it : " When the *a priori* yields nothing, it may be well to revert to observed facts. . . . When we examine the fundamental facts of human nature, when we regard the economic motive in its simplest terms, in order to discover whether prices are likely to rise or fall as activity is increased, nothing whatever is vouchsafed us. . . . Those theorists who seek to make economics more scientific by eschewing the uncertainties which are necessarily attached to empirical methods are in fact taking the path which leads away from science to pure scholastic." [64]

Before there can be any more " realistic " analysis some idea must be formed of what the more realistic assumptions are on which it is to be based,[65] unless deductive theorists are simply going to continue building up their analysis on any assumptions—say as to the wage-policy of trade unions when there is a rise in prices—which appeal to them impressionistically *a priori*, or which are " tractable " ; that is, make possible a fascinating display of mathematical or geometrical ingenuity, or which merely fit in with their political views.[66]

The objection has been made to statistical investigations, questionnaires to consumers and entrepreneurs, the examination of family budgets and the like, that the results of such arduous researches are subject to a high degree of inaccuracy, can easily be " cooked ", and in any case would not tell us much that we did not know already. The answer to such an objection is quite simple. If, as one is perfectly free to do, one considers that the results obtainable by the only possible scientific method open to one are not of sufficient interest to reward the effort of the investigation, then one must give up the scientific handling of these problems altogether and leave them to others of different intellectual tastes.

## NOTES

1. Cf. A. C. Pigou, *Economics of Stationary States*, p. 4.
2. Cf. A. Fey, *Der Homo Oeconomicus in der klassischen Nationalökonomie*, p. 122.
3. Cf. J. Robinson, *Economics is a Serious Subject*, p. 10.
4. Cf. P. N. Rosenstein-Rodan, *Economica*, 1936, p. 279.
5. Cf. J. Bentham, *Works*, edited Bowring, vol. i. p. 1. Cf. also J. Bonar, *Philosophy and Political Economy*, p. 225 : " But the older Utilitarians were bound by their principles to assume that the individual was infallible in following his interest " ; and the similar criticism of W. R. Sorley, *History of English Philosophy*, p. 223.

6. Cf. D. Ricardo, *Principles of Political Economy and Taxation*, ch. iv. In a passage most illuminating for his methods and postulates and scientific criteria, Ricardo does appear explicitly to make the " perfect expectation " assumption : " The first point to be considered is, what is the interest of countries in the case supposed ? The second, what is their practice ? Now it is obvious that I need not be greatly solicitous about this latter point ; it is sufficient for my purpose if I can clearly demonstrate that the interest of the public is as I have stated it. It would be no answer to me to say that men were ignorant of the best and cheapest mode of conducting their business and paying their debts, because that is a question of fact not of science, and might be urged against almost every proposition in Political Economy " (*Letters of Ricardo to Malthus*, ed. Bonar, p. 18). The only possible interpretation of this passage which might be paralleled in the writings of the Physiocrats, seems to be that economists are not to concern themselves with what actually happens in the economic world, as this is simply a question of fact, and not of science. The *scientist* assumes that people are omniscient as to their interests and are out to maximise their money returns, and deduces conclusions dependent on these and other such postulates. Where we agree with Ricardo is that " almost every proposition in Political Economy " conforms to his notions of a scientific proposition.

7. Cf. J. S. Mill, *Essays on Some Unsettled Questions*, p. 138.

8. Cf. J. Robinson, *Economics of Imperfect Competition*, pp. 241-2.

9. Mr. G. F. Shove explicitly introduced expectations into some formulae for the theory of value without discussing the conception at any length (*vide Economic Journal*, 1930, pp. 97-8).

10. Cf. J. R. Hicks, *Zeitschrift für Nationalökonomie*, 1933, p. 445, and Rosenstein-Rodan, *op. cit.* p. 271.

11. Cf. F. H. Knight, *Risk, Uncertainty and Profit*, p. 268.

12. Cf. R. von Keller, *Die Kausalzusammenhänge in der Konjunkturbewegung*, pp. 15-16.

13. Cf. *vide infra*, Section 5.

14. Cf. J. Robinson, *op. cit.* p. 15.

15. Cliff Leslie (*Essays in Political and Moral Philosophy*, p. 229), and later some of the Institutionalist critics, came very near to exposing this limitation in the " orthodox " Theory of Value. Cf. Z. C. Dickenson, *Economic Motives*, pp. 240-46 : " When we come to the market-place we find dealers absorbed in calculations which are reasoning, discovery, invention, rather than choosing

among utilities. Their desire to make the largest profit possible, within the rules of the game, is fairly constant ; the problem is *how* to make it. . . . As we have reiterated in many connections there is no *a priori* rule as to the accuracy for any individual's calculations. None can be completely accurate, for nobody knows *all* the consequences which will follow from any of his acts. Each of us is liable to be deceived as to the durability or stylishness of the clothes we buy. If any theorems of the accepted economic principles are dependent on the assumption of human infallibility in inferring the ultimate consumption utilities from concrete goods . . . of course those theorems are doomed." Cf. also T. Veblen, *The Place of Science in Modern Civilisation*, p. 227.

16. Cf. P. Wicksteed, *The Common Sense of Political Economy*, p. 121.

17. Cf. N. Senior, *Political Economy*, 6th edition, pp. 26-8.

18. Cf. W. S. Jevons, *Theory of Political Economy*, p. 18.

19. Cf. H. H. Gossen, *Entwicklung des Gesetzes des menschlichen Verkehrs*, p. 3.

20. The doctrine of Opportunity Cost is often expressed in a way which seems tacitly to postulate perfect foresight. The cost, it is said, to Robinson Crusoe of a hammer was the amount of fish he could have caught with the same expenditure of effort ; or the cost of the satisfaction from sixpence worth of cigarettes is the satisfaction one might have got from sixpence worth of chocolate, etc. "Còst here, as anywhere, means nothing but advantages to be derived from the use of given resources in other directions " (F. A. von Hayek, *Collectivist Economic Planning*, p. 6). But since the resources are never used in the other directions, how, failing perfect foresight, can one *know precisely and for certain* what they would have yielded ? How can Robinson Crusoe ever do more than make a forever unverifiable guess at what the "cost" of his hammer was ? that is, how much satisfaction his fish, whatever number he would have caught, would have afforded him. Failing some sort of perfect knowledge, what *would* have happened if someone had acted differently can only be the subject of speculation. For this reason the conception, *ex post*, of maximising returns is practically of little significance. It obviously has little or no sense to say that any particular individual, Lord Nuffield, the local greengrocer, or the winner of the Irish Sweepstake "maximised their returns ".

21. Cf. J. M. Keynes, *General Theory of Employment, Interest, and Money*, pp. 139-40. In a footnote Mr. Keynes asks the question, " But was he [Marshall] not wrong in supposing that the

marginal productivity theory of wages is equally circular ? " Since any purely theoretical deduction *as such* must necessarily be circular, the charge of "circularity" appears usually to mean that the assumption is untrue and unrealistic and the theory therefore inapplicable. In this sense the marginal productivity theory of wages would appear to be less "circular" than the marginal productivity theory of interest, since the assumption that the marginal productivity of the worker is equated to the wage would appear to be more probably generally true than that the marginal productivity of capital is equated to the rate of interest, *because the former can more easily be done.* Workers on short contracts can quickly be taken on or thrown off to adjust a divergence between the wage and marginal productivity, but such adjustments cannot be made with capital sunk in machines of long life. On the other hand, to judge from the following quotation, the assumption of the marginal productivity theory of wages (*i.e.* correct expectations as to the productivity of labour) is as unlikely and difficult as that of the marginal productivity theory of capital, which is therefore no more " circular " than the marginal productivity theory of wages : " The judgment or estimation as to the value of a man is a probability judgment of a complex nature, indeed. More or less based on experience and observation of the outcome of his predictions, it is doubtless principally after all simply an intuitive judgment or 'unconscious induction', as one prefers " (F. H. Knight, *op. cit.* p. 229).

22. Cf. J. M. Keynes, *op. cit.* p. 141 ; also G. Myrdal, *Beiträge zur Geldtheorie*, ed. F. A. von Hayek, p. 394.

23. Cf. L. Schönfeld, *Grenznutzen und Wirtschaftsrechnung*, p. 6. Cf. also G. Mackenroth, *Theoretische Grundlagen der Preisbildungsforschung und Preispolitik*, 1932, p. 134 ; O. Morgenstern, *Wirtschaftsprognose*, p. 36 ; and P. N. Rosenstein-Rodan, article " Grenznutzen " in *Handwörterbuch der Staatswissenschaften.*

24. The very term " utility " is ambiguously used for *both* ex-ante desire measured by demand price, *and* ex-post satisfaction, as though the two necessarily correspond. Professor Pigou (*Economics of Welfare*, 3rd edition, p. 24), mentioning that lack of correspondence between the two might have great practical importance, concludes that in fact it has not, and may be disregarded (except for the well-known case of the underestimation of future satisfactions, to compensate which he proposes State action). He would thus appear to be making what amounts to an assumption of roughly perfect expectation.

25. Cf. L. Schönfeld, *op. cit.* p. 28.

26. Cf. F. H. Knight, *Essays in Honour of Cassel*, p. 330, and L. M. Fraser, *Economic Thought and Language*, p. 177.

27. Cf. F. H. Knight, *Risk, Uncertainty and Profit*, p. 197 ; J. R. Hicks, *op. cit.* p. 445 ; A. C. Pigou, *op. cit.* p. 76.

28. Cf. O. Morgenstern, *Zeitschrift für Nationalökonomie*, 1935, p. 337 ff.

29. Cf. J. M. Keynes, *Treatise on Money*, vol. i. p. 176.

30. The contradiction in this procedure emerges clearly from Professor Knight's discussion of static equilibrium. On pp. 76-7 (*op. cit.*) his marionettes start as " normal human beings . . . familiar in a modern Western nation . . . acting with ordinary human motives . . . knowing what they want and seeking it intelligently ". But by p. 268 they have become, as quoted above, " mechanical automata ".

31. We may say at once that, though it may be difficult to find a precise and satisfactory definition, we do not regard the proposition " A expects or believes x " as being not conceivably testable, and therefore on our standards extra-scientific. See below, V. 3.

32. Cf. O. Morgenstern, *op. cit.* p. 354.

33. Cf. J. M. Keynes, *op. cit.* p. 156.

34. Cf. A. C. Pigou, *op. cit.* pp. 87-8. The emphasis in recent years on the unity of the Theory of Value under competitive and monopolistic conditions and the uniformity of the basic assumptions is apt to conceal the fundamental distinction between competitive and monopolistic conduct, or conduct " heeding " or " heedless " of rivals.

35. This conclusion would appear to be in correspondence with the conclusion that under monopolistic conditions there is no determinate equilibrium. Cf. A. C. Pigou, *op. cit.* p. 227, and H. von Stackelberg, *Marktform und Gleichgewicht*, pp. 94-8, *et passim.* The conception of equilibrium as essentially a *competitive* equilibrium in the classical writers, and J. B. Clark, for example, was *logically* sound, though the idea of some force breaking down all monopolies in the long run was *empirically* far-fetched.

36. Cf. J. Robinson, *op. cit.* pp. 21-3 ; and on the other hand E. R. Chamberlin, *Theory of Monopolistic Competition*, pp. 31 and 46, and H. von Stackelberg, *op. cit.* pp. 86 ff.

37. *Vide supra*, Section 2.

38. This is apparently what Edgeworth had in mind when he said that normally under monopoly there is not a sufficient number of conditions to render economic equilibrium determinate, and that in a world of monopolies there would be no occupation

for abstract economists, who would have to make way for em-
piricists (cf. *Collected Papers*, vol. i. pp. 136-8). J. S. Mill in an
interesting passage may have been making the same point :
" . . . only through the principles of competition has political
economy any pretension to the character of a science. So far as
rents, profits, wages, prices are determined by competition, laws
may be assigned for them. Assume competition to be their exclusive regulator, and principles of broad generality and scientific
precision may be laid down according to which they will be regulated. The political economist justly deems this his proper business:
and, as an abstract of hypothetical science, political economy
cannot be required to do, and indeed cannot do, anything more "
(*Principles*, People's Edition, p. 147).

39. Cf. J. R. Hicks, *op. cit.* p. 445 : " Die Vorbedingung für
Gleichgewicht in diesem weitesten Sinne ist *vollständige Voraus-
sicht.* Ungleichgewicht ist somit die Enttäuschung der Erwar-
tungen." But if complete expectations cannot be disappointed,
" undisappointed " expectations may very well be incomplete.
See also the quotation in the next note but one.

40. By an endogenous change we mean a change in people's
market behaviour ; by an exogenous change, which of course will
often be correlated with an endogenous one, any other type of
change. It is not clear whether changes in individuals' holdings
of cash, or in their " monetary " conduct, is " endogenous " or
" exogenous ", but this lack of clarity does not affect greatly our
use of the term here. See the discussion in G. Haberler, *Prosperity
and Depression*, pp. 8-10.

41. Cf. F. A. von Hayek, *Economica*, p. 41 : " Correct foresight
. . . is a defining characteristic of equilibrium ".

42. Cf. F. A. von Hayek, *op. cit.* p. 43. Cf. also E. Lundberg,
*The Theory of Economic Expansion*, p. 2.

43. Cf. F. H. Knight, *op. cit.* p. 152.

44. Cf. J. B. Clark, *The Distribution of Wealth*, pp. 279 and
408-9, by whom this rather question-begging comparison was
often used.

45. Cf. L. Robbins, *Nature and Significance of Economic
Science*, 2nd edition, p. 102.

46. Professor von Hayek (*op. cit.* p. 49) appears to hold, on
the other hand, that the assumption of a tendency towards
equilibrium is true in the former significant sense, *i.e.* that we are
usually in, or interestingly near, equilibrium.

47. Cf. E. Lundberg, *op. cit.* p. 24.

48. Cf. J. M. Keynes, *op. cit.* pp. 162-3.

49. Cf. M. Schlick, *Fragen der Ethik*, p. 27 ff., on the *Motivationsgesetz*.

50. Cf. G. Myrdal, *op. cit.* p. 437.

51. Cf. A. C. Pigou, *op. cit.* pp. 87-8.

52. For the relation between falsifiability and empirical content cf. K. Popper, *Logik der Forschung*, pp. 13 and 43. Popper brings out very clearly that it is the function of a scientific law to "forbid" some conceivable types of occurrence : " Nicht umsonst heissen die Naturgesetze ' Gesetze ' : Sie sagen umso mehr, je mehr sie verbieten ". A circularity or tautology " forbids " nothing. It is " true " whatever occurs, and therefore empirically empty. Cf. also C. G. Hempel and P. Oppenheimer, *Der Typusbegriff im Lichte der neuen Logik*, Leiden, pp. 105-6 : " Typologische Systeme, in denen keine denkbare Mischform der zugrundegelegten Typenmerkmale als empirisch ausgeschlossen bezeichnet wird, enthalten überhaupt keine empirischen Gesetze und haben daher nicht den Charakter wissenschaftlicher Theorien ".

53. Cf. D. Ricardo, *Letters to Malthus* (ed. Bonar), p. 18 n.

54. Cf. L. von Mises, *Grundprobleme der Nationalökonomie*, pp. 32-3 and 139, and J. Robinson, *op. cit.* pp. 211-12.

55. Cf. L. von Mises, *op. cit.* p. 50.

56. Cf. L. Wittgenstein, *Tractatus Logico-Philosophicus*, p. 167.

57. Cf. L. Robbins, *op. cit.* p. 93.

58. Cf. M. Bowley, *Nassau Senior*, pp. 43-8. Dr. Bowley emphasises the similarity between the doctrines of Senior—" the most important writer on scope and method among the classical economists "—and the contemporary doctrines of Professor von Mises and his followers.

59. Quoted by Cliff Leslie, *op. cit.* p. 202.

60. F. Lutz (*Das Konjunkturproblem in der Nationalökonomie*) brings out very clearly the point that there can be no deductive theory based on assumptions of mistaken conduct, but he comes to exactly the opposite conclusion to us that a theory of the trade cycle and fluctuations must be constructed on an assumption of rational unmistaken conduct—implying presumably perfect expectation. We cannot help fearing that such an attempt is bound to lead to the dilemma of the classical economists who set out to examine the problem of " overproduction " on the tacit assumption that no such thing could occur.

61. *Nationalokonomisk Tidskrift*, 1935, p. 191.

62. *Literary Remains*, p. 568, quoted by H. Wagenführ, *Der Systemgedanke in der Nationalökonomie*, p. 160.

63. Cf. G. Haberler, *Prosperity and Depression*, p. 242.

64. Cf. R. F. Harrod, *The Trade Cycle*, pp. 38-9.

65. O. Morgenstern, *Zeitschrift für Nationalökonomie*, 1935, p. 356, and C. F. Roos, *Dynamic Economics*, p. 68.

66. *Vide* Appendix for examples of " political " assumptions.

Without entering into the particular criticisms of different accounts of the rate of interest with which it is concerned, the following general criticism of impressionist assumptions in dynamic theories makes some very relevant points : " It is impossible to over-emphasise the truism that existence and non-existence of an effective discount of the future remain nothing more than tentative postulates, until appropriate statistical analysis establishes the one or the other postulate as a fact. For generations followers of the classical doctrine have *assumed* that time-preference is a strong determinant of saving and dis-saving ; now Mr. Keynes *assumes* that time-preference is not important as a determinant of dis-saving and new savings. These conflicting opinions are both based only upon intuition and personal experience, which are at best untrustworthy criteria, and the more so when in conflict. Both Mr. Keynes and the classicists seem to have fallen prey to what has, in another connection, been called the ' Ricardian vice'."—G. R. Holden, *Quarterly Journal of Economics*, 1938, p. 294.

# V

## INTROSPECTION, UTILITY, AND THE "PSYCHOLOGICAL" ELEMENTS IN ECONOMICS

1. *" Les sensations sont donc intransmissibles, ou plutôt tout ce qui est qualité pure en elles est intransmissible et à jamais impénétrable. . . . La science, en d'autres termes, est un système de relations. Or nous venons de le dire, c'est dans les relations seulement que l'objectivité doit être cherchée ; il serait vain de la chercher dans les êtres considérés comme isolés les uns des autres."*

HENRI POINCARÉ
La Valeur de la Science

2. *" A scientific theory that is incapable of experimental testing is valueless."*

L. S. STEBBING
A Modern Introduction to Logic

## INTROSPECTION, UTILITY, AND THE
## " PSYCHOLOGICAL " ELEMENTS IN ECONOMICS

### 1. THE " PSYCHOLOGICAL METHOD "

BEFORE proceeding further it is necessary to discuss here a doctrine which seeks to give to the propositions of Economics a significance quite unique among the sciences, which no other scientists appear, to-day at any rate, to claim for their propositions. This doctrine goes back at least as far as Senior and Cairnes, was advocated influentially by Wieser who called it the psychological method, and plays an important part in various modern methodological writings.[1]

Senior, recently shown to be one of the most important contributors to orthodox economic methodology, held that economic propositions were arrived at by pure deduction from premises consisting of " a very few general propositions, the result of observation, or consciousness, and scarcely requiring proof, or even formal statement, which almost every man, as soon as he hears them, admits, as familiar to his thoughts, or at least included in his previous knowledge ".[2] He gave a list of four of them.

Cairnes went further : " The economist starts with a knowledge of ultimate causes. He is already, at the outset of his enterprise, in the position which

the physicist only attains after ages of laborious research. . . ." He is " already in possession of those
ultimate principles governing the phenomena which
form the object of his study . . . since we possess direct
knowledge . . . of causes in our consciousness of what
passes in our minds ".[3]

According to Wieser : " We can observe natural /
phenomena only from outside, but ourselves from
within ". The employment of this inner observation
is the psychological method, " which finds for us
in common economic experience all the most important facts of economy. . . . It finds that certain acts
take place in our consciousness with a feeling of
necessity. . . . What a huge advantage for the
natural scientist if the organic and inorganic world
clearly informed him of its laws, and why should we
neglect such assistance ? " [4]

Contemporary writers do not appear essentially
to have modified these doctrines, though giving them
an important anti-empirical turn by urging that these
propositions " logically precede all experience and are
a condition and assumption of all experience ",[5] and
by giving them the name of " *a priori* facts " (" not
objective facts ").[6]

It is possibly very encouraging for the economist
to hear that compared with the natural scientist the
psychological method saves him " ages of laborious
research ", but it is curious and a pity that this huge
start has not enabled him to formulate any considerable body of reliable prognoses such as the natural
sciences have managed to achieve. Even so, it could
be argued that the propositions which this psychological
method affords us possess a necessary, certain, and
*a priori* character which those of the natural sciences

can never attain to. But it is strange, again, that psychologists and sociologists do not appear to have any inkling of this secret or make any such claims for their propositions. It is high time to find out precisely what these important propositions are.

This, unfortunately, it is not very easy to do. For though their certainty and their " *a priori* " and labour-saving characteristics are given great emphasis, an extensive search in the literature of the last twenty to twenty-five years has not yielded any precise, clear, and exhaustive list of these scientifically unique propositions. Presumably they are so obviously and necessarily true that it would be redundant even to write them down. But just to satisfy the pedantic claims of scholarly completeness one might expect, here and there, to find a list of them.[7]

However, it is possible from hints and references, particularly in Senior and Cairnes, to gather what the most central of these propositions are, even if one is not to be provided with a precise formulation. The first is that which in the previous chapter we called the Fundamental Assumption or " maximum principle ". We may pass over the fact that many of those who to-day advocate " the psychological method " would not agree with Cairnes' hedonist formulation that the economic subject acts " from a desire, for whatever purpose, to possess himself of wealth ", which throws rather a light on the accuracy of that " feeling of necessity in our consciousness " of which Wieser spoke. We have seen in the previous chapter that, unless we make definite postulates as to expectations which would beg the questions at issue, the Fundamental Assumption yields no very significant conclusions, that it is

133

difficult to formulate it clearly as an empirical generalisation that is not at any rate sometimes false, and
that as a definition it is highly inapt, and in any case
says then nothing about how people do in fact behave.
This first case does not strike us as very likely to
save " ages of laborious research ".

The second definite example of these propositions
is Gossen's Law, or the law of diminishing marginal
utility. As Wieser put it : " Within us the process
occurs, which is the content of Gossen's Law, with a
feeling of necessity. . . . Without induction we have
from the evidence of our inner experience the knowledge of a law which we know we have to assume as
effective in all cases." [8]

From time to time there have been considerable
controversies [9] as to how precisely " this familiar and
fundamental tendency of human nature ", as Marshall
called it,[10] should be formulated, and particular exceptions to it have even been urged, for example the
enjoyment of a piece of music. Leaving these difficulties, which may be surmountable, on one side, we
notice that more than one economist does not appear
to have experienced as he ought to have done the
" inner feeling of necessity " : " The Law of Diminishing Marginal Utility is a most insecure foundation. It
is at best an unproved hypothesis, obtained by an
amateur incursion into the domain of psychology." [11]
Further Professor Schumpeter, against whom, specifically, Wieser's criticism of "naturalism" was directed:
Gossen's Law " is not a law of Economics . . .
but an assumption based on an empirical economic
generalisation. As such it is therefore in principle
arbitrary. We could, for example, make the opposite
assumption, and it could not be called false." [12]

We are not at all concerned necessarily to advocate this latter conception of Gossen's Law. On
the contrary, in denying that Gossen's Law is a
" law ", Professor Schumpeter appears to be making
use of the concept of law against which we argued in
a previous chapter. All we want to do is to enquire
of those who hold to the " psychological method " of
" *a priori* facts " as to what tests they have for justify-
ing their propositions against such criticisms. If one
conceives of Gossen's Law as an empirical generalisation one can, when one wants to, go to the facts of
economic behaviour to test it. On the other hand,
simply to rely on dogmatic assertion even when supported by phrases like " inner feelings of necessity "
and " *a priori* facts ", is to commit scientific suicide.
It must really be explained in what precise way this
" inner feeling of necessity " with which the psychological method justifies its propositions differs from
the " inner feeling of necessity " which political
fanatics and the like always discover in support of
their doctrines. There is certainly no more readiness
on the part of the economists for the essentially
scientific intersubjective appeal to fact, for " these
propositions logically precede and are the condition
of all empirical facts ".

There is, thirdly, what has been called " the Principle of Scarcity "—" der Tatbestand der Lebens-
not " [13] (we may overlook the possible complications
in the Principle introduced by the existence of in-
voluntarily unemployed resources). Sometimes this
is referred to as " an empirical accident ", but by
some it would be regarded, apparently, as one of these
" *a priori* facts ". In any case it is difficult to see
why it is vastly more certain and necessary than any

obvious facts of natural science. It would seem occasionally to come to be used dangerously like a definition. Nevertheless it can be framed so as to possess empirical content, and how it could be falsified is the theme of all dreams of a *Schlaraffenland*, a land of Lotos-eaters where there are free goods to satisfy all desires and infinite " world enough and time " to enjoy them.

The only objection is that from this fact of scarcity *alone* nothing significant can be deduced as to how creatures confronted with this fact will organise their economic life. Animals are confronted with " the fact of scarcity ". It may have been imagined that, *given* a certain social and technical environment—which is already, it could be argued, far too large a " gift "— together with the "Fundamental Assumption", "the principle of scarcity " will yield the rest. But this is not so. As we have seen, a further and fatally question-begging assumption about people's expectations and knowledge must be made.

It is necessary for those who still advocate this possibly misleadingly-named procedure " the psychological method ",[14] to make two points clear which up to now are highly obscure : *first*, very precisely what these propositions are, so that it can be seen whether any significant deductions can be made from them alone ; *secondly*, how the truth of them can be tested in a scientifically respectable way.

Our conclusion, for the reasons given above, is that we are dealing here with a confusion between the *a priori* and introspection—two concepts which themselves are certainly obscure enough to permit of such a confusion—and further with a lack of clarity as to the precise content of the " Fundamental Assumption ". This is supported by "the all too human love of certainty ", and an urge to exalt the certainty and inexorable necessity of the propositions of Economics above those of the natural sciences.

In Wieser's presentation particularly, a very sharp distinction, on which the whole argument appears to turn, is drawn between " inner " observation or introspection and " outer " observation, and on this distinction some fundamental difference between the methods and criteria of the natural sciences and those of the " moral " sciences is based. This distinction we must now examine more closely.

## 2. INTROSPECTION

What is meant by the process of introspection would appear to be something as follows. An economist, A, over a period of time considers the marginal utility to him of possessing different amounts of money income. He finds, over a certain range, that the marginal utility to him of money income declines the larger its amount. He can formulate his conclusion by writing down the law of diminishing marginal utility of money for economist A.

If he is concerned to arrive at results of general application, and is not concerned simply to construct an economic science of himself, he cannot stop at this stage. But plainly he cannot get any further by " introspection ". With regard to the diminishing marginal utility of money he has discovered all he can by introspection. It is a meaningless contradiction to talk of introspection into someone else. Similarly unless A is the only economist—the only person in the world interested in the marginal utility of different amounts of money income—his results can only be accepted as observable behaviour or written or spoken words by his fellow economists, since obviously the notion of other people introspecting into A is likewise nonsensical.

It is sometimes suggested that he must now take a wild leap into the blue, and, without further ado, generalise his result by assuming that everyone is like him in this respect. This is something as though an astronomer said, " I know what our planet is like, I shall assume that all other planets are inhabited in the same way ", without enquiring about the matter further. This is obviously a hopelessly unscientific procedure which may well lead to definitely erroneous results. Moreover, if he does make such a wild assumption he must tell us how conceivably it can be tested, that is, he must indicate under what conditions it would be true or false, or else his assumption is illegitimate since it is not conceivably testable. Moreover we know that everyone is *not* alike in all the respects on which such assumptions may be made—for example, their desires for different goods under different conditions. There are perhaps certain broad similarities between people with regard to their desires and satisfactions, but the problem is just what these similarities are and how far they go. It is certainly not at all clear how a *scientist* can enjoy a " pacified professional conscience " while basing his procedure on a marginal utility curve drawn up on the assumption that " other people have much the same psychology as himself ", for which proposition no conceivable method of testing is given except " blind faith " (cf. theosophists).[15] It is curious also that some economists who recommend this procedure for drawing up marginal utility curves challenge the very same assumption as " illegitimate " or " normative " when it is required for " proving " that an equal distribution of money income maximises " social utility ".

The economist must clearly take some further step if he is to generalise his proposition concerning the diminishing marginal utility of money. This is sometimes very crudely, but sufficiently for our purpose, described as follows. Having examined by introspection the marginal utility of different amounts of money income to himself, he perceives that this " inside experience " is correlated with a certain " external " behaviour of his as regards money income. He arrives at the conclusion by " external " observation that his " external " behaviour regarding money is similar, in general, to everyone else's. He assumes or draws the analogy from this, therefore, that everyone else is " internally " similar to himself.

We again leave on one side the difficulty as to how this " internal " assumption could conceivably be tested. This is connected with the crudity of the distinction between " inside " and " outside " experience. At this stage we want simply to emphasise the more obvious point that our economist cannot get any general results by introspection alone, but only by observation of " external " behaviour (which may be so delicate as tone of voice, or facial expression), spoken and written words, etc., but which (to continue with this crude and misleading distinction) must be " external ", whether further inferences or analogies as to the " inner " experience are drawn or not. Further, as the individual introspecting economist is but one, and as he wants results applicable perhaps to many hundreds, thousands, or millions, it is the recording of " external " behaviour which must furnish an overwhelming part of the evidence.

One cannot " feel " (*einfühlen*) oneself or draw analogies into the blue. There must be some " behaviour " on which to hinge these psychological associations. Words such as " satisfaction ", " annoyance ", and so on, are in fact so used that we verify the presence or absence of these " emotions " in other people by observing the human body.

We do not wish to become involved in any general discussion as to whether the various processes called *einfühlen* and *verstehen* are or are not useful, significant, or legitimate. These seem to be just the kind of issues over which methodologists and philosophers argue for decades, but the result of which never affects or seems likely to affect any concrete scientific problem—the theory of the trade cycle or monopolistic competition or public finance. We conclude simply that, so far as these processes—we must confess to being not absolutely precisely clear as to what is meant by them—are simply used for making a scientific exposition more graphic and understandable by playing on the psychological associations of the reader, they may well be exceedingly valuable. It may well also be invaluable for the scientist engaged in the preliminary thinking-out of a hypothesis to imagine himself in the place of, say, a trade union leader or a Central Bank director, though this is simply a *Gedankenexperiment* which must be followed up and tested by " field " investigation. Thus used, these processes can never lead to serious or lengthy controversy. It is clearly a more or less psychological or even aesthetic question as to which method of presentation is the most effective, or a psychological one as to which is the best method of thinking out valuable hypotheses. But this has no more to do with the scientific content of the finished propositions than has the kind of type in which they are printed, or whether the scientist stimulated his brain before formulating them by means of coffee or alcohol.

But if it is imagined that the *Einfühlung* somehow actually adds something of scientific content, something which can conceivably be tested as " true " or " false ", here it must be pointed out that, on our conception, *Einfühlung* (for which term like *verstehen* there is no translation) begins precisely where the conceivably testable propositions as to people's behaviour, speech, writings, etc., leave off, and if the door is now opened to propositions that can never conceivably be brought to any kind of inter-subjective empirical test, but at the same time are supposed to have some kind of scientific validity, the progress of economic science will constantly be obstructed by all sorts of controversies, interminable in their very nature, and there will be no effective barrier against pseudo-science.

We are not here limiting any conceivable field of study or excluding any conceivable problems ; we are simply proposing the enforcement of certain criteria for the scientific investigation of any field and any problems, and showing how in fact the discovery of an economic law—the law of diminishing marginal utility—can be and must have been perfectly well carried out consistently with the strictest upholding of these criteria.

With regard to the trustworthiness of propositions

recording the results of introspection [16] we may allude to maxims like Goethe's " We know ourselves never by reflection but by action ", and Nietzsche's " Jeder ist sich selbst der Fernste ". We may mention, also, that modern psychologists appear particularly to warn against people's own too facile accounts and explanations of themselves as being infected with self-justifying " rationalisations ". Other sciences, further, where possible do not place much reliance on introspection. A doctor, even when treating himself, would not take any serious action simply on his own feelings of a temperature, but would rather use a thermometer on himself and trust his " external " observation of the thermometer, which may conceivably not be working properly. It appears, therefore, a misuse of terms, to put it mildly—if this was really what was ever meant —to say that introspection yields " *a priori* facts ".[17]

We conclude then that " introspection ", in the sense in which we have described it—the term may be used in other senses,—is not really a rival to empirical observation, and that to compare them as two methods and conclude that one is superior to the other is misconceived. They are not on the same plane at all, being applied at different stages of the formulation of scientific propositions, and in their respective places, empirical observation is quite obviously indispensable, and introspection very probably so. No scientist can rely on introspection alone if he wants results of general applicability, while he can only communicate the results of his introspection—leaving out of account telepathy and thought-reading—by his behaviour or his written or spoken words. Though, on the other hand, he could *conceivably*, if scarcely in practice, dispense with introspection entirely, it is certainly an invaluable and in fact practically indispensable method for the forming of general hypotheses about one's fellow human beings to observe, first, from a peculiarly intimate but not necessarily more trustworthy or accurate position, oneself—though all such hypotheses must afterwards be tested by empirical investigation.

In conclusion, in case it is necessary, we wish to emphasise that this analysis of " introspection " is in no way to be confused with the doctrines of solipsism or Behaviourism. In so far as these doctrines say either " Only I am conscious " or " Consciousness does not exist ", not only do we refrain from any such assertions, whatever they may mean, but we should ourselves be inclined to use the word " conscious " in a way which would render such propositions quite certainly empirically false. We have, in any case, not been concerned to establish any proposition about the " existence " or " non-existence " of something, but solely to analyse language and definitions, and to uphold the Scientific Principle of Testability. Of course if one rejects this principle such analysis as this has no significance.

### 3. " EXPECTATION ", " UTILITY ", AND " SOCIAL UTILITY "

Concepts like " wages ", " prices ", and " money " are sufficiently clear-cut never to give economists much difficulty. Even with concepts like " saving " and " capital " which give rise to considerable logomachy, the ground under one's feet feels perfectly firm ; the difficulty is where, precisely, or on exactly what ground one is. But in dealing with concepts like " expectation ", " utility ", and " social utility " many economists perhaps have been haunted now and then by a tinge of uneasy suspicion as to whether they were still on terra firma at all. The faint haze or mist which seems to surround these concepts has been responsible perhaps for the uneasy feeling of " that elusiveness which seems to inhere in concepts involving subjective valuation ",[18] which has brought about the custom of qualifying the use of such concepts with cautionary phrases like " if this is a legitimate concept ".[19] Our aim in this section is to try and dispel, somewhat, these unpleasant associations.

Whether a concept is " legitimate " or not depends first on one's criterion of legitimacy, and secondly on one's definition of the concept. We have outlined in previous chapters our criterion of legitimacy, so the problem remains simply whether we can conveniently and usefully define these concepts in accordance with it. No sign or word is, as it were, somehow stamped from birth as illegitimate, " unscientific ", or nonsensical ; if it *is* this, it is because of the definition we choose or refuse to give it.[20] We particularly emphasise this point, because the discussion of these concepts is so often carried on in the thoroughly misleading " material " mode instead of in the more precise "formal" mode.[21] " There is no such thing ", we are told, " as a comparison of utilities ",[22] or " A general price-level does not exist ". This looks as though some empirical proposition is being stated which might conceivably be false ; for example, " There are no such things as black swans ". But here it is not a question of some conceivable " thing " or " procedure "—" a comparison of utilities ", or " a general price-level " which as a matter of fact, search where one will, could not be discovered anywhere however perfect one's statistical resources are and however one could manipulate them. The proposition that " There is no such thing as a comparison of utilities or a general price-level " amounts simply to " We do not choose to give these concepts any scientific meaning ", or " As a convention we regard it as empty and useless ".

Taking the concepts " expectation " and " utility " first, we have no hesitation in defining these concepts legitimately according to our criterion. That is, propositions such as " A gets utility from a good " or " A expects a rise in prices " can quite conceivably be tested empirically, and we can indicate what must be the case if they are true. We could test such propositions by exposing A to certain stimuli, asking certain questions under certain conditions, and observing his reactions.[23] One can, if it is useful—at present it does not appear to be so particularly,—make these concepts more precise by laying down more precise tests and conditions, and reactions and answers on A's part.

Such results are not " absolutely certain and conclusive " because, to put it in the rough " material " mode, " absolutely certain and conclusive tests do not exist ", or, in the more precise formal mode, " absolute certainty and conclusiveness " have no sense as applied to empirical synthetic propositions. Of course, further, there is a " conventional " element as to what tests, conditions, and reactions one lays down—just as there is fundamentally a conventional element, if one cares to use the term (we do not know precisely what is the meaning of a " non-conventional element " in a definition) in precisely defining *any* concept or proposition. To say that any such definition may not get at the " real ultimate " utility or expectations seems as gratuitous metaphysics as to hold that some particular definition *does* attain this.

When, therefore, it is argued that one cannot observe utility or what a man expects or thinks, if this means that propositions like " A expects a rise in prices " or " A gets utility from this or that commodity " are not conceivably testable, we reject this argument and prefer the ordinary usage by which such propositions are regarded as definitely verifiable or falsifiable. If it is replied that this usage is vague and ambiguous, then it must be pointed out that it is precisely the task of science to make vague concepts more precise. *A fortiori* we reject the argument that because they make use of such concepts as these there is some fundamental difference in method making it impossible for the procedure of the social sciences to be assimilated to that of the physical sciences.[24] If, on the other hand, such concepts are not or cannot be defined in accordance with our criterion, we reject them for *any* science, social or otherwise, since we propose that the barrier against any sort of inconceivably testable utterances and therefore against pseudo-science must everywhere be rigidly upheld.

In dealing with the concepts of " social utility " and of " a comparison of utilities " the discussion may be made more precise by relating it to a particular proposition. Let us take, then, the assumption required—among others—for proving that an equal distribution of the social income maximises " social utility ". That is : " Equal amounts of money income yield equal utilities to different people ".

One *can* refuse to grant this the status of conceivably being a " scientific " proposition (in our sense).

One *can* hold that there are no conceivable conditions under which one could say this was true or false, and, obviously, that it cannot be deduced directly by pure logic or mathematics from any proposition of which this could be said. One might be given the example of a pair of twins who, when given or deprived of different amounts of income, or when tested with any other stimuli, responded with exactly similar words, gestures, and facial expressions, and whose brains and bodies when dissected, X-rayed, and so on, were found to be in exactly the same condition. One can then, if one likes, choose *not* to apply the proposition, " These two people receive equal utilities from equal amounts of income ", to this case. The argument advanced would probably be to the effect that " there is no objective criterion of utility " ; that this sentence deals with " feelings "—some " plus " behind all observable behaviour ; and since these, by definition, cannot be expressed in a sentence that is conceivably verifiable, the proposition about the twins, and *a fortiori* our initial assumption, does not fulfil our requirements for a scientific proposition. It is to be noticed that this argument is fundamentally concerned simply with a point of vocabulary—one proposes not to use the two sentences we have taken as examples in a way that will satisfy our requirements for a scientific proposition. At bottom, *given* the scientific criterion, propositions and concepts fulfil this criterion if we *choose* to define them as doing so, and do *not* fulfil it if we do *not* choose.

What is to be emphasised is that the rejection of our two propositions is going against the ordinary use of words, and is arguing in favour of some different usage. Ordinarily, if one asks people how they know that a man gets utility out of a commodity, or how

147

they know that one man gets more utility out of a commodity than another (for the whole of this argument can be applied to any proposition about an *individual's* utility, as well as to *comparisons* of utility),[25] one will probably not receive the answer " I haven't the faintest idea, there are no conceivable means of knowing ", but probably something to the effect that " This man regularly spends a greater percentage of his income on this commodity than the other ", or " When I asked them how they liked this commodity this man exclaimed in one way, the other in another way ". *That is what is called in ordinary language* " one man getting more utility out of a commodity than another ". Of course, whether the answers take exactly this form or not is irrelevant. The point is that one will be given an indication of some conditions which render the proposition true or false. If there was a bet on the subject, some test or criterion of " one man liking this commodity more than another man " would be agreed upon without any difficulty. The proposition would not be treated as some kind of metaphysical or emotional exclamation for which no intersubjective conditions of truth or falsity could be given.

*This is how words are in fact used*, and herein lies the core of truth in the common-sense " comparison of utilities ". As such analysis as this is so often misunderstood, we venture to repeat yet again that we have not been concerned with any conceivably verifiable or falsifiable empirical proposition that something is or is not practically possible, but only with the analysis of definitions and concepts and the upholding of the Principle of Testability.

It is perhaps indicative of more than a simply

superficial contradiction that those who seek to exclude " Welfare " Economics and Public Finance from economic science, one minute say that " there is no such thing as a comparison of utilities ", and the next that we are in fact making such comparisons every day.[26] To say that such a usage represents just an indirect *pis-aller* for finding out about people's utilities seems a curious use of words, since one has defined as inconceivable any " direct " method of verifying such propositions—any introspection into somebody else's mind. One cannot very sensibly call a road an " indirect *pis-aller* " when one defines as *inconceivable* any other road.

It might be argued, though it would involve a misunderstanding of the use of language, that, for example, a millionaire may " *really* " get much more (or less) utility from an extra shilling to his income than a beggar, though it cannot conceivably be observed in their speech, behaviour, attitude to money, or any other conceivably verifiable " external " way. Similarly one can argue that " really " no individual ever gets any utility out of anything, or that everyone in the world is going round with excruciating toothache but will never " show " it by behaviour, words, or the condition of the teeth, etc. But arguments of this kind are at once to be excluded as unscientific (in our sense), for *on their own definition* they are resorting to propositions the truth or falsity of which makes no conceivable observable difference, and which are not deducible from any scientific proposition. They are also, incidentally, arguments which would lead doctors— if it can be imagined that they would ever be taken in by such meaningless nonsense—to destroy their thermometers, since these cannot tell us anything about the " real " feelings or " real " state of health of their patients.

This medical analogy is perhaps of some force. When it is said that A is " in better health " now than a year ago, or in better health than B is, or that the standard of health of a class or nation is higher than it was twenty years ago, it would be a fantastic interpretation to say that these were some kind of not conceivably testable " value judgments " or ethico-metaphysical ejaculations.[27] If necessary they could be translated into more precise but much lengthier propositions about people's temperatures, blood conditions, hearts, livers, physique, death-rates, and behaviour. It is necessary to insist that those who put forward such propositions should always be ready, ultimately, to state precisely how they would test these propositions in such terms, and that they certainly should not indulge in controversy over them without being able to indicate these tests unambiguously.

Undoubtedly some economists who follow the very earliest traditions of the science as a science of wealth would find some such concept corresponding to "health", or the "standard of health", of great value for Economics and would perhaps find the most significant and interesting division of economic studies in examining the effects of different economic organisations and policies upon it. It is possible that " standard of living " might be an apter name for this concept than " social utility " or " welfare ", but we are concerned not with such finer terminological points but with the issue of principle as to the legitimacy according to our criterion of such a concept, label it how one will.

It is, then, perfectly possible and consistent with

150

the usual use of language to define the concept of the
comparison of the utilities of different individuals in
a scientifically legitimate way. We are concerned
here simply to establish this, rather than to lay down
what precisely would turn out to be the most useful
definition. One might make a definition of the proposition " Equal amounts of money income yield
equal utilities to different people " roughly as follows :
We say the N individuals of a community C receive
equal utilities from equal amounts of income, if,
when lined up and exposed to a certain list of stimuli
(questions, giving and taking away different amounts
of income, etc.), they all react in a similar way. It
would certainly be very difficult with our present
knowledge to verify this assumption, which may well
be far from the most useful formulation. It may also
appear very improbable that it would prove true.
But such objections can hardly be raised by any
economic theorist who makes use of " static " communities, with one homogeneous factor of production,
perfect expectation, perfect competition, and the like.
In fact compared with assumptions such as these it
would appear to possess something of an advantage
as a model for analysis. We have a certain number
of statistics available which let us know roughly how
fantastically " unrealistic " the assumptions of static
equilibrium are, but in this field of economic psycho-
physiology most of the facts remain to be discovered.

It may well be undeniable that vague " blanket "
terms like social utility, welfare, and so on have often been
very misleadingly used and left hopelessly undefined.
But it does not seem the best way of pointing this out
to say that " there is no such thing as a comparison of

utilities" or that this involves an unscientific "value-judgment". It may quite probably turn out, also, that a number of differently defined concepts of different "standards of living" may be more serviceable than the single and often much misused "social utility".

Certainly, further, there is a considerable element of convention in such definitions (and our formulation is probably an unnecessarily clumsy one). But if such a convention appears useful it is a quite misplaced desire for rigour and "exactness" that would exclude it provided it is logically unimpeachable. It would be just as sensible to object that "there is no such thing as brachycephaly or dolichocephaly since the way of measuring it is purely conventional"— as, of course, it is.

Nor is it in "welfare" economics alone that some such conventional concept is desirable. For example, some such conventional concept as a "general level of prices" is obviously of great value for the theory of index numbers and of money. To say "there is no such thing as the general level of prices", though it may help to correct misinterpretations of index numbers, is, as we have seen, at bottom only a confusing way of saying that one does not choose to adopt a convention which would almost certainly prove useful.[28] Just as in this case increasing statistical investigation ought to yield an index number that will better serve this conventional purpose, so in the case of our definition increasing investigation ought to yield much more useful concepts of the "standard of life". There is always a vital distinction between a proposition which owing to the nature of our present knowledge of the subject matter can only be put forward in the most tentative way, and a proposition which can never con-

*ceivably* be shown to be true or false. The tentativeness of the former may vanish with a further two or three hundred years of investigation ; the latter can *never* be of any use to a scientist.

There is, then, a logically sound peg on which to hang " welfare " analysis, which can thus be just as " positive " as the other parts of Economics (and being " positive " can never yield any " normative " conclusions). The concept, whether one calls it "social utility" or "welfare", or "the social standard of living ", can always ultimately be given an empirically ascertainable content even if this is for the most part held in the background simply for " shorthand " reasons. There is no question of large parts of " welfare " economics and Public Finance " going by the board", or suddenly collapsing before a philosophical pin-prick. For the objections to " welfare " economics consist in taking the word " utility " out of its everyday use, giving it some kind of scientifically unusable " definition " (or saying that it is " indefinable ", whatever that means), and then concluding that since " welfare " economics needs this concept it must be scientifically disreputable.[29]

## 4. " NORMATIVE " AND " POSITIVE "

The discussion of the concepts with which we have just been dealing—" welfare ", " social utility ", " comparisons of utility ", and so on—are often quite unnecessarily mixed up with controversies over " normative " and " positive " propositions, and " normative " and " positive " sciences. As Schlick made clear, " the whole conception of a contrast between normative and positive sciences is fundamentally false ",[30] and for scientists at any rate the controversy must be very nearly played out. For *any* empirical " science " we propose only the criterion of conceivable empirical testability. This we are never prepared to relax. There is, of course, no reason why propositions which take the form " such-and-such a measure will have such-and-such effects or fulfil such-and-such ends ", should not fully satisfy our criterion.[31] One may also even—though it is arguable that it is dangerous—make use of " normatively " tinged words like " optimum population " and " optimum firm ", provided a precise empirically ascertainable content is given—for example, "having minimum average costs ". If one likes, further, to say that propositions of this form are " normative " one may, but it is not clear what sense such an adjective would have, and there is certainly no fundamental distinction between these "normative" propositions and the ordinary "positive" propositions, since the one will always be exactly translatable into the other.

As Otto Neurath points out, it is not necessary always to take the use of the imperative in scientific works at once too tragically, even if its use is sometimes accompanied by irrelevant emotional suggestions.[32] Cookery books are usually worded in the imperative—" to make rice pudding take " . . . (cf. " to maximise the national income take " . . .), while chemistry books are usually worded in the indicative or conditional. But it is clear that the scientific content of the two types of book is logically similar, and the scientific content of a cookery book can always at once be translated into the indicative or conditional. Such formulations ought not to lead to untoward controversies, and so long as these are avoided, little can be said against the occasional use of such a mode of expression.

## NOTES

1. Cf. L. von Mises, *Grundprobleme der Nationalökonomie*, pp. 18-22, and L. Robbins, *Nature and Significance of Economic Science*, 2nd edition, ch. iv.

2. Cf. N. Senior, *Political Economy*, 6th edition, p. 5.

3. Cf. J. E. Cairnes, *Character and Logical Method of Political Economy*, pp. 83-90, and the quotation given by L. von Mises, *op. cit.* p. 20.

4. Cf. F. Wieser, *Gesammelte Abhandlungen*, p. 17.

5. Cf. L. von Mises, *op. cit.* p. 22.

6. Cf. F. A. von Hayek, *Economica*, 1937, p. 36, and *Collectivist Economic Planning*, p. 11 : " The essential difference is that in the natural sciences the process of deduction has to start from some hypothesis which is the result of inductive generalisations, while in the social sciences it starts directly from known empirical elements " (cf. L. von Mises, *op. cit.* p. 22, " *nicht* Erfahrung im Sinne der Erfahrungswissenschaft sondern gerade das Gegenteil davon ") " and uses them to find the regularities in the complex phenomena which direct observations cannot establish ".

7. A rough list (" ziemlich alles ") of these propositions is given by H. Mayer, *Zeitschrift für Volkswirtschaft*, 1911, p. 199. It corresponds, apparently, to the three propositions we consider above.

8. Cf. F. Wieser, *op. cit.* p. 29.

9. Cf. the controversy between F. Čuhel and Böhm-Bawerk, *Zur Lehre Bedürfnisse*, pp. 299-301.

10. Cf. A. Marshall, *Principles of Economics*, 8th edition, p. 91.

11. Cf. F. C. Benham, *Economica*, 1930, p. 184.

12. Cf. J. Schumpeter, *Wesen und Hauptinhalt der theoretischen Nationalökonomie*, p. 74.

13. Cf. L. Robbins, *op. cit.*, 1st edition, p. 96, and R. Strigl, *Die Ökonomischen Kategorien*, p. 14.

14. " Psychological " here means employing this special kind of economists' psychology, not specialist Psychology, for as Wieser said (*op. cit.* p. 16), " We are psychological laymen *and wish to remain so* ". (Our italics.)

15. Cf. J. Robinson, *Economics of Imperfect Competition*, p. 213.

16. It is important to distinguish analytically between the *proposition* " I am satisfied ", which may be made with any sort of expression, and which can be tested *intersubjectively* as to its truth or falsity, and a simple exclamation of satisfaction which cannot conceivably be " true " or " false ", though anyone can make true or false propositions concerning such exclamations. A *proposition* recording the results of introspection must, according to our criterion, be conceivably verifiable or falsifiable by other scientists. When a doctor takes his own temperature is this " introspection " or " outer observation " ?

17. Cf. K. Popper, *Logik der Forschung*, p. 56 : " Es ist ein verbreitetes Vorurteil, dass der Satz : ' Ich sehe, dass der Tisch hier weiss ist ' irgendwelche erkenntnistheoretischen Vorzüge aufweist gegenüber dem Satz ' Der Tisch hier ist weiss '. Aber deshalb, weil er etwas über ' mich ' behauptet, kann der erste Satz vom Standpunkte einer objektiven Prüfung nicht als sicherer angesehen werden, als der zweite Satz, der etwas über ' den Tisch hier ' behauptet."

18. Cf. L. Robbins, *Economic Journal*, 1934, p. 4.

19. Cf. W. B. Reddaway, *Economic Journal*, 1936, p. 419.

20. Cf. M. Schlick, *Philosophical Review*, 1936, pp. 339-69, and L. Wittgenstein, *Tractatus Logico-Philosophicus*, p. 129.

21. See above, II. 2.

22. Cf. M. S. Braun, *Theorie der staatlichen Wirtschaftspolitik*, p. 41 : " Eine Vergleichbarkeit von Gefühlsgrössen verschiedener Individuen gibt es nicht ".

23. Cf. L. Robbins, *Nature and Significance of Economic Science*, 1st edition, p. 123.

24. Cf. L. Robbins, *op. cit.*, 2nd edition, p. 89.

25. The apparently commonly held " middle " position rigorously excluding (a) welfare economics and public finance as " unscientific ", but, on the other hand, urging the use of (b) " psychological elements " to " explain " economic phenomena, and the emphatic rejection of some rather unspecified doctrine referred to as " Behaviourism ", is not an easily tenable one. It is both or none. No argument for the rejection or retention of convention (a) will hold very much water which does not imply necessarily the corresponding rejection or retention of convention (b).

26. Cf. L. M. Fraser, *Economic Thought and Language*, pp. 88-9.

27. Cf. Otto Neurath's pamphlet, *Was bedeutet rationale Wirtschaftsbetrachtung ?*

28. Cf. G. Haberler, *Festschrift für Spiethoff*, p. 95 : " Man macht die Sache nur noch schlimmer, wenn man wie Mises und

Budge, die Möglichkeit der Messung des Geldwertes prinzipiell leugnet. Denn hinter der angeblichen Unmöglichkeit, den Geldwert zu messen, verbirgt sich nur das Unvermögen, ihn überhaupt zu definieren oder anzugeben, was darunter zu verstehen ist."

29. Many would argue that it is some kind of " welfare " economics, largely statistical, that holds the future. Cf. M. Dobb, *Political Economy and Capitalism*, pp. 321-2 : In a socialist community " Clearly there will exist a class of problem to which the title economic statistics could, perhaps, most suitably be given. Already to-day there are studies which seem to furnish a prototype of what such a fuller science will be. I refer to such enquiries as the nutrition and family budget, population, and productive-capacity studies which are assuming a growing importance, and which are already passing beyond the preliminary stage of pure description to the construction of elementary generalizations, competent to form the germs of a future science."

30. Cf. M. Schlick, *Fragen der Ethik*, p. 14.

31. A good summary of the normative-positive aspects of science is given by E. Lindahl (*Die Gerechtigkeit der Besteuerung*, pp. 2-3) as follows : " Wir wollen in unserem praktischen Leben gewisse Zwecke verwirklichen und suchen nach den Mitteln zur Erreichung dieses Zieles. Dabei bewerten wir die Erscheinungen : je nach dem verschiedenen Grade, in dem sie unseren Zwecken entsprechen, erhalten sie für uns einen grösseren oder geringeren Wert. Diese teleologische Auffassungsweise muss aber auf die kausale begründet werden. Eine richtige Wertschätzung gewisser Erscheinungen als Mittel zur Erreichung eines gewissen Zieles setzt offenbar die Kenntnis der Bedingungen voraus, unter denen dieses Ziel zu erreichen ist. Die praktische Aufgabe der Wissenschaft ist dabei, den objektiven Kausalzusammenhang zu erklären, um uns den besten Weg zur Verwirklichung unserer Ziele zu zeigen. In dieser Weise wird die Wissenschaft die unmittelbare Grundlage unserer praktischen Handlungen sein. Sie wird ein mächtiger Faktor in der Regulierung unseres praktischen Strebens, ohne dabei ihren objektiven Charakter einzubüssen." Clearly Max Weber was making the same point when he spoke of science as " Technik ".

32. *Op. cit.* p. 11 ; cf. also K. Menger, *Morale, Wille, Weltgestaltung.*

# VI

## CONCLUSION

1. " *Es war für mich eine schöne Zeit, als ich meiner Fantasie freien Spielraum lassend Schlüsse auf Schlüsse baute und immer zu neuen Entdeckungen fortschritt. Aber ich bemerkte zu meinem Leidwesen, dass alles, was ich auf diese Weise schuf, in seinen Endresultaten doch nie mit der Wirklichkeit übereinstimmen konnte. . . . Als ich dies klar erkannt hatte, legte ich mir das harte Gesetz auf, mit dem Fortschreiten in den Ideen inne zu halten und alle Kraft und Zeit auf die Forschung der Wirklichkeit zu verwenden.*"

J. H. VON THÜNEN
Quoted by E. Schneider
Jahrbuch für Nationalökonomie u. Statistik,
1936

2. " *Economic dynamics will, in its entirety, incorporate into itself historical economics. The changes that are going on in the world will in future be studied inductively, as well as deductively; and it is the inductive part of the work that falls to the historical economist. In the long run it is this part that will need to absorb the most scientific labour. The static laws of economics ought, consequently, to be known at an early date.*"

J. B. CLARK
Distribution of Wealth

3. " *It is my view that the analytical method in the line of Ricardo, Mill, and Marshall has, for the time being, at any rate, reached the limit of its usefulness, and that no striking advance can be made thereby from the ground now occupied.*"

J. STAMP
Economic Factors in Modern Life

4. " *Until economic science is much farther advanced, ' economic principles' are less important to the economists than the reciprocal bearings of economics and the results of the other social sciences. Many economists are paying no attention to such interrelations, for mastering of them is a long and fatiguing task requiring an extensive knowledge of facts ; whereas anyone with a little imagination, a pen, and a few reams of paper can relieve himself of a chat on ' principles'.*" V. PARETO
The Mind and Society

5. " *It is important to know the language of size, because entrusting the laws of human society, social statistics, population, man's hereditary make-up, the balance of trade, to the isolated mathematician without checking his conclusions is like letting a committee of philologists manufacture the truths of human, animal, or plant anatomy from the resources of their own imaginations.*"

L. HOGBEN
Mathematics for the Million

# VI

## CONCLUSION

### 1. SUMMARY

WE began by laying down in the Introduction the criteria to which this book was to try to hold and in accordance with which it sought its solutions (I. 1-4). In the following chapters we made the following terminological proposals, and tried definitely to establish the following facts in accordance with these criteria. We proposed :

(1) That propositions used in economic science could conveniently be classified according as to whether they were or were not conceivably falsifiable by empirical observation (II. 1) ;

(2) That " propositions of pure theory " is a name for those propositions not conceivably falsifiable empirically and which do not exclude or " forbid " any conceivable occurrence, and which are therefore devoid of empirical content, being concerned with language. We noticed inductive confirmation of this analysis (II. 2-3) ;

(3) That in spite of an apparent confusion between what was called the " hypothetical experiment " and the laboratory experiment of natural science, the propositions of the " hypothetical " method were simply " propositions of pure theory " (II. 4) ;

161

(4) That "ceteris paribus" propositions are frequently hopelessly ambiguous and that the ceteris paribus assumption should be used less often and more cautiously (II. 5);

(5) That it involves a misconception of the task of a science to call propositions of pure theory "Laws", which is the dominant conception of Economic Laws throughout the history of Economics. To the formulation of this type of laws certain definitions of the subject matter of Economics wish apparently to restrict economists (III. 1-2);

(6) That it is hardly surprising, therefore, that every prominent economic theory has at some time or other by a sound authority been shown to be "circular", "tautological", or to "beg the question" (III. 1);

(7) That propositions of pure theory, by themselves, have no prognostic value or "causal significance" (III. 3);

(8) That the "optimistic" procedure seemed suddenly to come to a dead end with static theory, and may develop into an excuse for more or less useless deductive manipulation, instead of the more tedious but necessary empirical investigation (III. 4);

(9) That the "Fundamental Assumption" has almost always been formulated so as only to be explicable if a further assumption of "perfect expectation" is made, which latter postulate assumes most or all economic problems out of existence (IV. 1-2);

(10) That to make particular assumptions about some kind of imperfect expectations is largely

question-begging unless supported by empirical investigation (IV. 2 and 7) ;

(11) That perfect expectation and "monopolistic" conduct by more than one individual in an interdependent system are logically incompatible (IV. 5) ;

(12) That with the assumption of perfect expectation falls also the assumption of some kind of necessary "tendency" to equilibrium (IV. 6) ;

(13) That the advocacy of the psychological method of "*a priori* facts" involves a confusion of the obscure conceptions of "introspection" and the "*a priori*" (V. 1) ;

(14) That "introspection", practically indispensable in its own place, is not a rival method to be contrasted with empirical observation but is on a completely different plane (V. 2) ;

(15) That concepts like "utility", "expectations", "social utility", "welfare", or "standard of living", though liable to be misused, may well be valuable to the economist and can be defined quite conveniently and normally in accordance with our scientific criterion, and that "normative" and "positive" distinctions in face of this criterion have little relevance for the scientist who holds to it (V. 3-4).

The following further conclusions are even more tentatively put forward. We have throughout constantly implied that, apart from pure Logic and Mathematics, scientific knowledge, explanation, and prognosis can only be based ultimately on empirical regularities. In Economics these will be certain regularities—very qualified and far from universal—

as to how, in different situations, consumers, entrepreneurs, advertisers, speculators, savers, trade union leaders, bank chairmen, finance ministers, and so on, react and behave. All economic problems, however much they may be formulated as problems of wages, money, interest, and the like, can be reduced to such terms. An economic problem is a problem as to how people behave. Equilibrium Economics describes a community without economic problems, because *so far as it affects him* everybody knows how everyone else is going to behave.

Advance in economic knowledge depends ultimately on discovering, however limited, provisional, and tentative they may be, such regularities, and if such discoveries cannot be made—and we reject such a pessimistic view—Economics as an empirical science can go no further.[1] No sort of deductive manipulation can ultimately get round the difficulties: " What is important to observe is that unless there are general propositions about particular matters of fact, and unless some of these propositions are both true, and are believed to be true, there can be no knowledge that is rightly called scientific ".[2]

Scientists in all departments have long been tending to abandon claims to " absolute truth ", certainty, and exactness for their conclusions, and if they wish for a justification beyond their own intellectual pleasure, or " science for science's sake ", they base it on the benefit their work brings to mankind,— its " fruit-bearing " characteristics.[3] If economists are once and for all going to abandon often completely misconceived notions and standards of the " exactness " and " necessity " of their conclusions, and strive, rather, after more practical and " realistic " applicability, they must be prepared to extend the range of their conclusions to include political and sociological factors, or to co-operate in formulating their conclusions with the specialists in these fields.

No one, statesman or individual, can act on purely economic advice. *All State economic policy involves politics*, and no separate economic advice or economic solution of a problem of policy is of any use until the modifications in it resulting from political factors have been worked out.[4] Economists rightly condemn politicians who frame economic policy purely with an eye to what is politically convenient without taking any account, or sufficient account, of economic effects. But purely economic advice, say, of " healthy deflation ", or intellectually fascinating schemes of monetary management which take no account of the political corruption, unrest, or even revolution which they may lead to, are equally one-sided and equally to be condemned. The *political* side of politico-economic problems is represented, sometimes, as the " weakness of politicians " in not putting through necessary but unpopular measures, or " rigidities " or " frictions ". That is, the difficulties are not faced at all ; it is implied simply that they ought not to be there. Only advice and policy which is based on an estimate of the political, sociological, and economic effects *together* of a policy or measure can be sensibly acted on. It is platitudinous for economists to emphasise that their advice and estimates are based purely on the prognosis of economic effects and to claim no further validity for them, but how often just for this very reason are they, as they stand, more or less useless, and being of purely academic interest, can only mislead and confuse practical men.

165

It is significant to notice that several great economists—Pareto and Wieser among " equilibrium " economists, and Max Weber among historical economists—have treated their work on Economics as essentially a preliminary to wider sociological investigations. We have seen that within Economics the " optimistic " procedure of beginning with highly simplified " isolated " abstractions, in the hope of gradually making these more " realistic " and applicable by removing the simplifying assumptions, is apt to come to a dead end, and that if one wants to get beyond a certain high level of abstraction one has to begin more or less from the beginning with extensive empirical investigation. It is the same with attempts to simplify inextricably interconnected social phenomena by " isolating " them into watertight " political " and " economic " departments. Exclusively " economic " conclusions are vitiated by the same neglect of relevant factors as is " static " economic analysis.

This is not to argue that the only useful work is the production of vast and comprehensive sociological treatises like *The Mind and Society*, but that any particular advice or estimate as to the effects of different policies with regard to a particular issue will only be useful when it is not exclusively economic but is politico-economic. Those who wish to arrive at propositions usefully applicable to policy must usually be considerably more than economists.

## 2. THE IMMEDIATE PROBLEM OF THE TRADE CYCLE

We have tried here always to keep as close as possible to particular scientific propositions and concrete problems, and to avoid methodological generalities. In conclusion, we seek to apply the analysis and distinctions we have been making to the immediate problem, or nexus of problems, which at the moment confronts economists theoretical and statistical, and which is variously referred to as the Problem of the Trade Cycle or Fluctuations, the Theory of Employment or Unemployment, " Dynamic " Theory, or the Theory of Money and Interest. A discussion of the differences and disagreements surrounding these problems may particularly suitably close this book, as these disagreements throughout the history of Economics—particularly in the Ricardo-Malthus over-production controversy, for example—and at least to some extent at the present day, represent fundamental methodological disagreement ; disagreement, that is, as to the basic procedure and postulates on which any economic analysis is to be carried on.

It would probably be agreed that the sometimes seemingly almost complete disagreement among economists as to the analysis, explanation, and policy as regards the Trade Cycle, is not " really " nearly so acute as it may seem at first sight. But even the appearance of disagreement is highly disconcerting and destructive of influence. How then can disagreement, both actual and merely apparent, be as far as possible removed ?

Scientific disagreement, apparent or actual, can only be of two kinds and must always ultimately and conceivably be removable.

(1) It can, first, be verbal. At the present time, discussion of the problems of the trade cycle, though not of the theory of value, is carried on in four or five almost completely different (English) languages or sets of concepts. Each of the leading investi-

gators has his own private terminology, and though each employs a certain basis of terms common to all economic scientists, all the crucial analysis is often carried on with particular private *ad hoc* concepts, and the equivalent translations of the terms of one language into the terms of the others are often quite unclear. Far from there being any movement to a recognised unified terminology, it would appear sometimes to be imagined that something new is discovered about the trade cycle or its causation if yet another new terminology is invented for discussing it, and new " Fundamental Relations " and " Equations " between the new terms are contrived, or that a simple re-christening of the facts to be explained in some high-sounding terminology constitutes a scientific explanation. All the same, when the new terminology has been set forth and in a later chapter one comes to the new " explanation " of the trade cycle, one finds that it curiously resembles the standard and long-familiar accounts of the facts of the trade cycle, ornamented with a few terminological novelties. In other cases, to explain a particular depression, the "theory" is abandoned altogether, and some quite other factors than those emphasised in it are introduced for the explanation ; [5] or some particular fact or correlation of facts receives all the emphasis and is labelled as the "*fundamental*" *determining or causal factor* to the exclusion of all others.

It seems reasonable to argue that a certain measure of terminological unification, so that all writers employed roughly the same concepts and recorded their conclusions in roughly the same language, would not only sweep away much or all of the *apparent* disagreement, but would assist in the further removal

168

of genuine disagreements by making them stand out precisely in isolation. This would necessitate agreement on a certain recognised vocabulary from which, for convenience' sake, redundancies and synonyms would be eliminated, and any private new terms would be put forward as suggestions for general scientific acceptance, and defined in terms of the recognised vocabulary. This would lead to the avoidance of the practice, not entirely non-existent at present, of introducing whole new vocabularies in which each new concept is defined in terms of one of the other new concepts, so that the precise relation of the whole or of any individual term to previous terminologies is often very difficult to find out exactly.

We have no idea at all as to whether there is or ought to be sufficient readiness for scientific co-operation and give-and-take, and to forgo, to some extent, private terminological preferences in the interests of a standard terminology recognised as that of economic science. Possibly the variety of private terminologies of Professor X, or Mr. Y, and their bands of " disciples " (a term peculiarly suggestive of religious sects), each talking in their own exclusive private languages, may be preferred. We simply suggest that it is obvious that there will never be substantial and clear agreement, and therefore scientific authority, until all scientific investigators begin to adopt approximately similar terminologies.

(2) The second possible source of disagreement is as to the postulates or empirical facts. There is a whole tradition in Economics for not taking such questions or disagreements at all seriously. Mere questions of fact are regarded as simply questions of data or assumption, not questions of *science* at all, and the accusation

of a mistake here might, as Ricardo put it, " be urged against almost every proposition in Political Economy ".⁶ If they are "plausible" and "tractable", only the *naïveté* of the plain man expects anything further of the assumptions or mere empirical facts that are used. Any deficiencies in " realistic " accuracy will, in accordance with the " optimistic " procedure, gradually be remedied somehow. But it is clear enough that at the present time the most far-reaching disagreements as to the analysis, explanation, and policy for the trade cycle are due to differences on simple but basic questions of fact—the wage policy of Trade Unions with rising or falling prices, the employment policy of entrepreneurs in face of different measures at different stages of the cycle, the behaviour of savers and investors in face of changes in the rate of interest or the price of consumption goods, and so on.

As we attempted to show in Chapter IV, the answer to such questions as these cannot be somehow *deduced* from some " Fundamental Assumption " or other. The result is that *a priori* theorists fall back often on any vague " plausible " impressionist generalisations which fit in with the rest of their " system ". One has only to take up some of the most prominent works of recent years, whose proclaimed purpose it is to " explain " the trade cycle or fluctuations in employment or unemployment, to find sweeping empirical generalisations based on what it seems " broadly reasonable to assume " on such questions as these, on which other investigators are making diametrically opposite generalisations, without one hint or suggestion of statistical confirmation anywhere throughout the book. On such questionable foundations elaborate—but, of course, circular—deductive structures are erected which are attacked and defended, not without vehemence, but certainly without a mention even of the desirability of reference to the empirical facts.

These questions of fact may be answerable by existing statistics, or by statistics which, though not existing, could with ordinary effort be obtained. In these cases there is clearly no reason for disagreement to continue. Unfortunately in many cases it may not be practically possible with the resources available to obtain the statistics necessary to settle the question one way or the other. But this is exactly the case in which any dogmatic or exclusive insistence on one view, and intolerance of others, is scientifically unjustifiable, and the inconclusiveness of the position must be admitted. The politician and man of action has to base his policies on unknowns, and to justify it he goes far beyond the facts. But surely the distinguishing characteristic of the *scientist* with a modicum of scientific caution and discipline is, that though he may hold his own conjectures and hypotheses, he does not argue over and intolerantly attack or defend conjectures which he cannot confirm or refute according to agreed scientific criteria.

It might be argued that in addition to these two types of disagreement (and the possibility of disagreement owing to a logical inconsistency or inconsistent use of language) there is a third possible source of disagreement. Two investigators may use precisely the same terminology and agree on precisely the same empirical postulates—statistically ascertained or not—but still not be in complete scientific agreement. They could further disagree, it might be urged, as to what was " causally " important. It would seem that possibly the majority of disputes and disagreements on the subject of the trade cycle deal with differences about " causes ", but we deny that this represents any special new source of disagreement beyond the two we have discussed, verbal and factual.

What is meant by such propositions as that " this event was the cause or an important cause of a particular depression or of depressions in general ", or the proposition that " it was not a cause but a symptom ", or that " though a minor cause there were other more fundamental causes ", is, as we have already complained, usually hopelessly unclear. Faced with the two propositions, " A caused the Trade Depression " and " A did not cause the Trade Depression ", to what *conceivable* (not necessarily *existing*) statistics would one go? How would one set about finding out which proposition was true and which false ? What conceivable empirically observable difference would the truth of the one as against the other make ? [7]

If the answer is none, or if no clear answer is given, such propositions cannot conceivably be scientific according to our criterion. As a matter of fact, statistical tests of such propositions are probably seldom *inconceivable,* though often so very difficult and inconclusive *practically* that such propositions can never be much more than conjectures which can hardly be advanced with any exclusive emphasis, nor hotly argued over and disputed with any profit or conclusiveness.

When, therefore, as has often been argued against some theories of the trade cycle, it is said that some theory does not " get at the real causal factors " but simply amounts to a description, it is legitimate to enquire of the propounders of such criticisms in what type of propositions their " causal analysis " would be presented, and how these propositions would conceivably be verified.[8] It is extremely difficult in the social sciences to give the terms " cause " and " effect " any precise meaning beyond " what precedes " and " what follows " in time, and in the more advanced natural sciences such vague concepts are displaced by that of functional dependence. Monocausal explanations of social phenomena are mostly recognised to-day as a certain sign of quackery or political fanaticism, trying to justify its prejudices by some simple but comprehensive " philosophy " of history or society, which reduces everything to a function of some one factor, say " race " or the technique of production.

All any *scientific* investigator can do to " solve the problem " of the trade cycle is to formulate as convenient and accepted a terminology as possible for discussing the facts, and use this in obtaining the fullest and most precise description possible of the facts, and, above all, of regularities and correlations in the facts. When he tries to go beyond this he will be advancing, we have argued, propositions which probably have no clear empirical content whatsoever, and which cannot be tested either by any statistics practically obtainable, or possibly even conceivably obtainable. Certainly in this field of vague conjecture bordering on metaphysics every kind of inconclusive disputation and interminable polemic is possible, and there is no reason for supposing that any kind of agreement will ever be reached.

173

Our " recipe " for agreement, therefore, on the problems of the trade cycle—if this agreement and synthesis is considered desirable—is as follows : (1) co-operation in working out an agreed unified terminology ; (2) co-operative statistical investigation as to all differences on empirical fact ; (3) restraint as to all arguments and assertions not practically supportable by statistical evidence, particularly when involving the terms " cause " or " effect ", which should not be used at all without an attempt to indicate a precise definition.

These conclusions are broadly very similar to those reached in the first great controversy on these issues by Malthus, with a quotation of whose words we may suitably close : [9]

" The principal cause of error, and of the differences which prevail at present among scientific writers on political economy, appears to me to be a precipitate attempt to simplify and generalise. While their more practical opponents draw too hasty inferences from a frequent appeal to partial facts, these writers run into a contrary extreme, and do not sufficiently try their theories by a reference to that enlarged and comprehensive experience which, on so complicated a subject, can alone establish their truth and utility. . . .

" The tendency to premature generalization occasions also in some of the principal writers on political economy an unwillingness to bring their theories to the test of experience. . . . The first business of philosophy is to account for things as they are ; and till our theories will do this, they ought not to be the ground of any practical conclusion."

# NOTES

1. E. Lundberg appears to be laying the same stress on *regularities* in the correlation of expectations and conduct when he writes (*Theory of Economic Expansion*, p. 175) : " It is sensible to link action with expectations only if the latter can be explained on the basis of past and present economic events. *Total lack of co-ordination here would mean the complete liquidation of economics as a science.*" (Our italics.)

2. Cf. L. S. Stebbing, *A Modern Introduction to Logic*, 2nd edition, p. 246.

3. Cf. B. Russell, *The Scientific Outlook*.

4. Cf. M. Weber, *Gesammelte Aufsätze zur Wissenschaftslehre*, pp. 168-9 : " Steht historisch fest, dass auf zwei in ökonomischer Hinsicht gleiche Situationen dennoch verschieden reagiert wurde, —infolge der Differenzen der politischen, und religiösen, klimatischen und der zahllosen anderen nicht ökonomischen Determinanten,—dann degradiert man, um die Suprematie des Ökonomischen zu erhalten, alle diese Momente zu den historisch zufälligen ' Bedingungen ', unter denen die ökonomischen Motive als ' Ursachen ' wirken. Es versteht sich aber, dass alle jene für die ökonomische Betrachtung ' zufällige ' Momente ganz in demselben Sinne wie die ökonomischen je ihren eigenen Gesetzen folgen, und dass für eine Betrachtungsweise, welche ihre spezifische Bedeutung verfolgt, die jeweiligen ökonomischen ' Bedingungen ' ganz in dem gleichen Sinne ' historisch zufällig ' sind, wie umgekehrt."

5. Cf. F. Lutz, *Konjunkturprobleme in der Nationalökonomie*, pp. 138-45.

6. Cf. IV. 1, above.

7. Cf. III. 3, above.

8. Cf. F. Lutz, *op. cit.*, for an example of this type of criticism (pp. 57-61).

9. Introduction to *Principles of Political Economy*.

# APPENDIX

## SOME POSTULATES OF ECONOMIC LIBERALISM

By the Classical Economists, and still authoritatively in recent years, it has been held that Economic Science quite definitely demonstrates that a Liberal, capitalist, *laissez-faire* economic policy leads to maximum returns for the community or to greater returns than any collectively planned economic policy. We refer to this doctrine as " Economic Liberalism ".[1] The examination of how such doctrines could possibly come to be held affords some further illustrations of the criticisms of economic method made in the previous pages. We present these here simply in so far as they tend to throw further light on the general arguments of this essay, without obviously in any way attempting a fuller examination of the Capitalist-Socialist issue. We are concerned simply with the significance of economic theory, and if the criticisms of this Appendix seem to deal mostly with one side of the issue, this is only because it seems to have been claimed mainly by one side alone that orthodox economic theory proves its case.

The marginal principle makes it clear that a society is, in a certain sense, in a " maximum " position when, on the one hand, all consumers so distribute their expenditure that no one can gain by transferring any of it from one commodity to another, and when on the other hand no producer can gain by transferring productive resources from one productive activity to another.[2]

The *societas economica* [3] strives always to be as near this position as possible, combined with stability through time— that is, a constant stable average is probably preferred to large fluctuations around the same average. If all members of the society had perfect foresight the striving for this position would present no problems, or, if so, problems of an entirely different significance from those that face any contemporary

177

community. The problem for any community like ours is, *given* the degree of imperfection of our foresight and our technical productive power, how can we so organise our economic life to be as near as we can to the ideal " maximum " position over the period of time and with the degree of stability we desire, and how, by organisation, can we improve our economic foresight (the problem for the economist) and our technical productive power and foresight (the problem for the technician)?

One answer or group of answers to this question is that called collectivist planning. We wish to examine the Liberal criticism of this answer first from the demand side with regard to the consumer, and secondly from the supply side with regard to the entrepreneuring function carried out under planning by some sort of centralised authority.

In discussing the concept " consumer's freedom of choice " the distinction must be emphasised between two extreme types of choice : between (1) choice between " absolute " *certainties, e.g.* choice between a piece of white bread and a piece of brown bread of given quality for immediate consumption, the " utility " of each of which can be " certainly " foreseen and compared by the prospective consumer ; and on the other hand (2) choice between absolute *uncertainties, e.g.* choice of the number on which to make an isolated bet, of a given sum, at a roulette table. Of course all, or nearly all, actual choices are a mixture, somewhere in between these two extremes of certainty and uncertainty, but this does not make the distinction any the less fundamental analytically.

As regards the second kind of choice, apart from the pure pleasure in gambling for its own sake, which we may leave out of account here, there is no advantage or significance at all in being free to make it oneself as against having it made for one. It would be quite reasonable to call " irrational " anyone who got no pleasure from pure gambling, but who in having an isolated bet to make on a roulette table minded whether he chose his number himself or whether somebody else chose it for him. There is no question of comparing the expected utilities of putting one's coin on No. 14 or on No. 15. The range of choice being confined to absolute uncertainties all choices are alike, and it is therefore irrelevant in what way they are made for one.[4]

When, therefore, it is said that in the capitalist market " each individual is at liberty to distribute his expenditure in such a way that he cannot gain by transferring money from one commodity to another ",[5] this freedom (and therefore this proposition) can hardly be said to have much significance in so far as expectations are imperfect. Such " liberty " is enjoyed by a man *forced* to gamble at a roulette table.

The term " absolutely certain " is not applicable, in principle, to any choices in this world, and therefore no choices belong fully to the first type above, however near to it a large number of them may lie. A large number of choices probably lies much nearer the second extreme type, and particularly, to judge from comparisons of the capital markets to casinos,[6] many of the choices of investments. But the distinction (of degree) between " certain " and " uncertain " choices by no means corresponds to the distinction (of degree) between choices from among capital goods and choices from among consumption goods, as some investments are highly " certain " in their return and some consumption goods highly uncertain. Liberals, however, seem sometimes to be tacitly assuming that all choices are of, or approximate very nearly to, the first " absolutely certain " type, just as we have found in Chapter IV. the ubiquitous implication of the assumption of perfect expectation, from Ricardo onwards, and less often its explicit statement. The misleading conclusion is therefore drawn that to take away from consumers the right to make a choice is always *necessarily and to the same extent* to take away from them some significant " freedom ".

But under conditions of uncertainty and imperfect foresight *richness* of choice (and therefore we suggest " *freedom* " in any significant sense) does not necessarily correspond with mere *width* of choice, but is a function also of foresight. When in England one may always go to an *à la carte* restaurant, but if abroad in the *à la carte* restaurants the menus are all printed in a language one cannot understand—even though one may be convinced that the average standard of the food may be quite as high or higher than in the *table d'hôte* restaurants—one may well prefer to make one's choice at a restaurant of the latter type—though it will be a far narrower choice, or no choice at all—if the menus there are printed in English. That is, people may well prefer an economic organisation which gives them a narrower range of choice if they can be more *certain* as to the returns from different choices.

One's judgment, therefore, as to the *richness* of choice in a capitalist society will depend very much on how far one considers the average member is possessed of the technical knowledge enabling him to judge correctly the returns from different choices—knowledge of food-values, wireless sets, tooth-pastes, and so on. It is a vastly complicated empirical question as to whereabouts between the two extremes of certainty and uncertainty most choices lie, and which choices could be centralised without loss of freedom. Sweeping (and tacit) assumptions one way or the other are obviously unjustifiable.

It is, though, perhaps interesting to call attention to certain phenomena connected with the making of choices as they actually occur in contemporary " capitalist " societies.[7]

In America, before 1929, which probably came nearer the freely competitive capitalist organisation than any other society of recent decades—though it was certainly far from the ideal—consumers' assistance bureaus were in existence whose purpose it was scientifically to analyse different products on the market—the chemical properties of different soaps, foods, and so forth—and to report to consumers. Foresight and knowledge were sold to consumers, who apparently, perhaps wrongly, thought it remunerative to buy it rather than trust either to themselves or to advertisements, the whole purpose of which, in so far as they are not purely informative, may be interpreted as that of making people's expectations *less* correct.

One finds in existence, too, experts for the purpose of advising on any large transactions—the buying of houses, cars, particularly second-hand ones, investments, etc.—sellers, that is, of foresight. Finally, most people who have the money to do so hire others—estate managers, housekeepers, and so on— to make their choices for them. Of course these experts are chosen and are dismissable by those who hire them, but that is what the experts of the central planning board would be in the social democratic Utopia.

It is therefore not the case that the planning authority

would necessarily not give people what they wanted, and force on them what they did not want—" *dictate* " to them, to use an emotionally tinged word with which Liberals make great play. The issue is whether the democratic planning authority will possess (1) technical knowledge sufficiently superior to the average consumer in a capitalist market as to what goods will best satisfy different *given* tastes and wants, and further (2) more good-will than the individualist capitalist producer in not deliberately trying to *deceive* consumers, as he is tempted to try by advertisements, etc., *which two superiorities will together make up* for the possible, but by no means necessary, inferiority of the planning authority to the individualist capitalist producer in its knowledge of the actual tastes and wants of consumers.

We certainly do not venture to generalise here on what is largely a *political* issue—the relations of democratic authorities and of experts to the general public. We emphasise that there is no legitimate *a priori* conclusion either way.

When we turn from the consumer to the entrepreneuring function we find the one-sided assumption of perfect expectation, which pervades and largely vitiates Liberal criticisms of collectivist planning as they stand, brought very explicitly to the front.

For example : under capitalist conditions, " if a new undertaking is planned, one can calculate beforehand whether and in what way it can be made to pay. . . . In the capitalist order of society it is easy to calculate which railway line is the most profitable. . . . The socialist authority, however, would be faced with a task which it could not possibly solve. It would not be in the position to decide which of an infinite number of possible procedures is the most rational. Thus the socialist economy would soon lead to general chaos, in which an irresistible and rapid sinking back to the primitive conditions of our forefathers would be bound to set in." [8]

Again : " The dictator will not even find that his plans are not upset by unforeseen changes, since the changes in tastes are by no means the only, and perhaps not even the most important, changes that cannot be foreseen. Changes in the weather, changes in the numbers or the state of health of the population, a breakdown of machinery, the discovery or the sudden exhaustion of a mineral deposit, and hundreds of other constant changes will make it no less necessary for him to reconstruct his plans from moment to moment." [9]

But in a capitalistic economy apparently, although " mistakes arise from the necessity of calculating with what are not from many points of view rigorously ascertainable data, . . . still, all such mistakes can be confined within certain narrow limits so that they do not disturb the net result of the calculation ".[10]

But why mistakes owing to the unpredictability of consumers' tastes and the weather should apparently give rise to important difficulties in a planned economy, but be " confinable within certain narrow limits " in a capitalist economy—unless one is tacitly slipping in the usual " equilibrium " assumption of perfect or nearly perfect foresight in a capitalist economy—is hardly clear.

This one-sided and therefore completely self-stultifying character of the postulates being made—a conspicuous example of assuming precisely what one has to prove—seems the only possible interpretation of such passages.

In a " dynamic " economic world many decisions cannot be simply *calculated* but must be based more or less on " intuition ",[11] and the whole issue turns on whether the socialist state official or the individual capitalist fulfils this entrepreneur function more successfully. It is not very convincing for anti-planners to prove that the individual capitalist is the better entrepreneur by, apparently, tacitly assuming a world of perfect foresight where no entrepreneuring (in the sense of adaptation to unforeseen and unforeseeable change, as against *organisation*) [12] is necessary, and where therefore the task, since there is none, must be perfectly carried out. The analysis is completely of a piece with Say's investigation of overproduction and his conclusion that there was no such thing. Equally unconvincing, if there is no political emotion on one's side to appeal to, are the airily confident generalisations of the planner unsupported by any agreed or concrete proposals for economic organisation.

Clearly the problems here, the efficiency of civil servants and so on, are to a considerable extent political questions, and equally clearly sweeping generalisations can hardly represent scientific conclusions but simply partisan feelings.[13] In this connection, however, it is interesting to notice the constant Liberal *motifs* of suspicion and contempt for the politician and civil servant and of the capacity of the voter to choose his representatives on the one hand,[14] and on the other hand implicit faith in the honesty and public spirit of the business man, who, if he attempts to deceive his customers, will at once be eliminated owing to the keen competition maintained by the intelligent consumers always on the watch for their economic interests.

Adam Smith spoke of " that insidious and crafty animal vulgarly called the statesman or politician ". Any very important distinction in tone in Professor von Mises' discussion of the civil servant is not easily perceptible.[15] On the other hand, in business, as Bentham put it, " the force of the social motives tends continually to put an end to that of the dissocial ones ".[16] It is well known that the Classical economists and J. B. Clark believed that competitive equilibrium was constantly being very nearly approached, and that there was a constant " natural " tendency to competitive conditions and the break-up of monopolies ; and if all consumers had perfect expectations no entrepreneur would dare to try and deceive them, and there would be no advertising. The Liberal tautology is that if people knew how to achieve maximum returns, wanted to do so, and were free from obstruction, they would in fact maximise their returns. At least one part of the assumptions usually left unstated is obviously false. Liberals are criticising or constructing economic policies on assumptions which make any policy at all absurdly superfluous.[17]

It seemed at first that Professor von Mises and his followers were attempting by purely theoretical arguments to prove some " impossibility " or " inner contradiction " in collectivist planning—and their methodological views would apparently support the feasibility of such an attempt. It is seen that on closer examination the issue remains the same as that of the old capitalism-versus-socialism controversies, of the incentives to efficiency under socialism, the dangers of bureaucracy, the position of artists under socialism, and such-like hoary problems. As the inadequacy of their purely theoretical condemnations becomes more apparent it is at this level that Liberal criticism comes more and more to end up. But, on such points as these despite the new material afforded by Russian Communist planning, have any new arguments been discovered which would not have been considered stale and inconclusive by a pre-war political debating society? Much stimulus has undoubtedly been given to the fruitful investigation of questions of socialist organisation, but it could have been done more directly than by the procedure—not unprecedented in the history of Pure Economic Liberalism—of advancing purely theoretical arguments based apparently on unstated, sweepingly one-sided, and empirically false assumptions.

It must always be remembered that *laissez-faire* and equilibrium doctrines had their origin in *rationalistic Utopia-building*.[18] Because the postulates of economic theories were not always emphatically and unambiguously made clear, the Utopia, under the unique conditions of economic expansion in population, geographical area, and investment of the early nineteenth century, somehow got mixed up with the mechanism of the economic world as it is, or as it approximately is, or even as it might be. It is high time to put these theories firmly back in their place as Utopian constructions.

## NOTES

1. Cf. the writings of the leader of contemporary Economic Liberalism, L. von Mises, *Kritik des Interventionismus*, pp. 23-4, *Liberalismus*, pp. 3, 78, and 170: "Liberalism is the application of the doctrines of science to the social life of men, to Politics. . . . Knowledge of Political Economy leads necessarily to Liberalism. . . . Liberalism and Political Economy were victorious together. No other politico-economic ideology can in any way be reconciled with the science of Catallactics. . . . One cannot understand Liberalism without Political Economy. For Liberalism is applied Political Economy, it is state and social policy on a scientific basis. . . . Liberalism starts from the pure sciences of Political Economy and Sociology, which within their systems make no valuations and which say nothing about what ought to be or what is good or bad, but only ascertain what is and how it

is. If this science shows that of all conceivable possible organisations of society only one, that resting on private property in the means of production, is capable of existing, because none of the others can be carried through, there is nothing in this which justifies the term optimism. . . . Science has succeeded in showing that every social construction which could be conceived as a substitute for the capitalist social order is in itself contradictory and nonsensical and could not work out in the way its advocates explained. . . . He who recommends a third type of social order, of regulated private property, can only deny the possibility of scientific knowledge in the field of Economics altogether." Cf. also W. H. Hutt, *Economists and the Public*, p. 367 : " Our plea is in short for that economic liberty which was dimly visualised by the Classical economists, and whose coincidence with the *summum bonum* has been an implication of the subsequent teachings of economic orthodoxy. We have attempted to show that expert, dispassionate and disinterested thought on these matters has been the preserve of those whose gropings in a world of divergent beliefs and arguments (beset on all sides by the lure of interests) have led them to the path of orthodox tradition."

2. With allowance for differences between the marginal private and the marginal social net product.

3. Cf. S. Helander, *Rationale Grundlagen der Wirtschaftspolitik*, p. 35.

4. A legitimate use of the Principle of Indifference. Cf. J. M. Keynes, *Treatise on Probability*, p. 309.

5. Cf. L. Robbins, *Planning and International Order*, p. 193.

6. Cf. J. M. Keynes, *General Theory of Employment, Interest, and Money*, ch. 12.

7. For an account of the consumers' advisory bureaus, the amazing composition and fraudulence of some of the best-known goods on the American consumption market, the methods of psychologically trained advertisers and the helplessness of the consumer in the heyday of American capitalism, *vide* S. Chase and F. J. Schlink, *Your Money's Worth, A Study in the Waste of the Consumer's Dollar.*

8. Cf. L. von Mises, *Liberalismus*, pp. 63-4, and *Collectivist Economic Planning*, ed. Hayek, p. 108.

9. Cf. F. A. von Hayek, *Collectivist Economic Planning*, p. 217, and also *Economica*, 1933, pp. 132-3 : " Closer analysis, however, reveals the fact that either of the alternatives which the intelligent planner is supposed to adopt would lead to a waste of resources, and that the wisest thing he could do would be to bring about by

delicate regulation what is accomplished spontaneously by competition ". It is not difficult to prove that planning could not possibly do better than the market mechanism, if one is assuming perfect expectation by everyone in the market ; otherwise there is a logical *non-sequitur* here. Cf. on the other hand, R. von Strigl, *Einführung in die Grundlagen der theoretischen Nationalökonomie,* p. 213 : " In der freien Verkehrswirtschaft werden Irrtümer und Fehler der Wirtschaftsführer ebenso zur Geltung gelangen wie in einer organisierten Wirtschaft ; die Unmöglichkeit einer völlig genauen Kalkulation ist in dem einen wie auch in dem anderen Falle gegeben ".

10. L. von Mises, *Collectivist Economic Planning,* p. 110. It is particularly curious to find taken as an example precisely that industry, " mistaken " investment in which is usually regarded as the cause of several of the slumps when Economic Liberalism was at the height of its ascendancy. Cf. L. Knowles, *Industrial and Commercial Revolutions,* p. 261 : " So little was known or realised as to the possibilities of railways that the prospectus of the Liverpool and Manchester Act said that the new railway held out ' a fair prospect ' of being a cheap and expeditious means of conveyance for travellers, the receipts from which were estimated at £10,000 a year, *an estimate which proved itself ten times too small* ". (Our italics.)

11. Cf. Keynes, *op. cit.* p. 163 : " We are merely reminding ourselves that human decisions affecting the future, whether personal or political or economic, cannot depend on strict mathematical expectation, since the basis for making such calculations does not exist ; and that it is our innate urge to activity which makes the wheels go round, our rational selves choosing between the alternatives as best we are able, calculating where we can, but *often falling back for our motive on whim or sentiment or chance* ". Also Roos, *Dynamic Economics,* p. 167 : " It is possible that some producers estimate values of production which maximise their profits per unit time, *but it is certainly not probable that the majority of producers estimate production rates anywhere near the maximising values.* There are too many variables, price, cost, consumer-income, etc., involved for producers to approximate the maximising values." (Our italics.) Cf. similarly Knight, *Risk, Uncertainty and Profit,* p. 293.

12. Cf. N. Kaldor, *Economic Journal,* 1934, pp. 70-71.

13. Cf. M. Dobb, *Review of Economic Studies,* vol. ii. p. 150 : " To speak of a competitive economy achieving the same result, if it had the same degree of foresight, is to ignore the fact that its

essential nature is that it does not and cannot possess the same degree of foresight"; and Hayek, *op. cit.* p. 225 : " If we abstract, as we are probably entitled to do, from the case where there is reason to assume that the planning authority possesses greater foresight and is better qualified to judge the probability of further technical progress than the individual entrepreneur. . . ." One cannot help remarking the dangerously easy transition from deductive theorising to dogmatic partisan debating on question-begging assumptions.

14. It is quite arguable, as Professor Hutt (*op. cit.* p. 262) says, " that consumers in the market-place are incomparably more rational and less seriously misled by propaganda than voters under representative government "; though this would seem a rather impressionist generalisation on which to build any scientific case. But this is not quite the relevant contrast. One may certainly say that voters are open to a lot of " irrational " and misleading propaganda, but even the greatest technical expert in politics could not frequently forecast and control events more successfully than an average " man in the street ", partly because political ends—what people really want to get by their political activity—are so very obscure, and partly because prognosis and accurate technical knowledge in politics is far more difficult to arrive at. It has been claimed, for example, that a completely " inexpert " and non-specialist man with ordinary common sense may make a far " more successful " Foreign Secretary than a specialist expert with a vast knowledge and experience of diplomacy and international law. This is far more doubtful of, say, a Central Bank director. The expert in politics cannot be so authoritatively equipped with technical knowledge superior to a man in the street as the chemist, dietician, mechanic, etc., who would be employed by the democratic planning authority to use their vastly superior technical knowledge to see that *given* wants were met by goods— food, clothing, soap, wireless sets, etc.—which the most expert scientific knowledge available to the community considered would be the most successful ; instead of the technically completely ignorant man in the street being left to himself and the advertiser. The case for an economic " government " more authoritative (though democratically controlled) than the political government rests on the superiority of the technician's knowledge as to the purely technical qualities of goods over the knowledge of the average man, a superiority far greater, it may be suggested, than that of the *political* expert's corresponding ability to forecast and control compared with the average man. The *absolute* difficulty of prognosis

and technical knowledge in the two spheres for both expert and non-expert is irrelevant.

15. It is difficult to see how the working classes can be expected to give an intelligent dispassionate vote considering Professor Hutt's gratuitous emphasis on the " lack of self-respect, the resentful or acquiescent inferiority complex of the working classes " (*op. cit.* p. 81). For Prof. von Mises on Bureaucracy, vide *Liberalismus*, p. 91. Professor Hutt gives a perfect example (*op. cit.* p. 104) of an economist making precisely those political assumptions which it is convenient for his doctrines to make. According to him civil servants would administer regulations of which he approves, (*e.g.* dissolving price corporations or preventing price discrimination) impartially, and " without risk of corruption ". If, however, any measure of which Professor Hutt does not approve but of which some socialist might approve (*e.g.* profit-fixing) was attempted, then " the dangers of corruption cannot be avoided at all ", and the position " would always be precarious ".

There is a danger to-day of the, in their time, liberal and progressive anti-politician and anti-bureaucrat slogans of Bentham and Adam Smith coming to sound too nearly in tune with those of every would-be dictator in Europe (cf. Mosley, " The corrupt old gang at Westminster ", and La Rocque, " Contre les politiciens ").

16. Quoted by S. Helander, *op. cit.* pp. 14 and 20.

17. Cf. the very apt comments of I. Sundbom, *Zeitschrift für Nationalökonomie*, 1937, p. 621 : " Bemerkenswert ist nun, dass diese wirklichkeitsfremde Abstraktion die Natur der Preisbildung repräsentieren soll und dass die anderen dynamischen Elemente nur als zufällige Störungen betrachtet werden. Dass in der Tat eine ökonomische Theorie ziemlich überflüssig wäre, wenn die Natur der Preisbildung durch die Gleichgewichtslehre zum Ausdruck käme, hat man nicht berücksichtigt. . . . Wenn wirklich die Preisbildung in Uebereinstimmung mit der Theorie funktionierte, so würden die meisten Schwierigkeiten, mit denen die wirtschaftliche Praxis zu kämpfen hat, von selbst verschwinden. Die beste Wirtschaftspolitik wäre, überhaupt keine Politik zu betreiben." As Sundbom interestingly points out, the early pioneers of equilibrium theory like Quesnay seemed to realise that the perfect harmony of the ideal economic system depended on omniscience—the omniscience of God—while human ignorance prevented the actual system attaining to the ideal. It was insisted, however, that the economist should concern himself with the divine harmony of the ideal system rather than with the imperfect

actuality. We do not know whether contemporary equilibrium economists would care to make use of this justification.

18. For the Utopian origins of *laissez-faire* doctrines, cf. S. Bauer, " Origine utopique et métaphorique de la théorie de ' laissez-faire et de l'équilibre ' ", *Revue d'Économie Politique*, 1931, p. 1589.

# INDEX OF NAMES

# INDEX

THE END